PHalarope books are designed specifically for the amateur naturalist. These volumes represent excellence in natural history publishing. Most books in the PHalarope series are based on a nature course or program at the college or adult education level or are sponsored by a museum or nature center. Each PHalarope book reflects the author's teaching ability as well as writing ability. Among the books:

THE AMATEUR NATURALIST'S HANDBOOK
VINSON BROWN

BOTANY IN THE FIELD: AN INTRODUCTION TO PLANT
COMMUNITIES FOR THE AMATEUR NATURALIST
JANE SCOTT

A FIELD GUIDE TO THE FAMILIAR: LEARNING TO
OBSERVE THE NATURAL WORLD
GALE LAWRENCE

THE PLANT OBSERVER'S GUIDEBOOK: A FIELD BOTANY
MANUAL FOR THE AMATEUR NATURALIST
CHARLES E. ROTH

SUBURBAN WILDLIFE:
AN INTRODUCTION TO THE COMMON ANIMALS
OF YOUR BACK YARD AND LOCAL PARK
RICHARD HEADSTROM

THOREAU'S METHOD:
A HANDBOOK FOR NATURE STUDY
DAVID PEPI

TREES: AN INTRODUCTION TO TREES AND FOREST
ECOLOGY FOR THE AMATEUR NATURALIST
LAWRENCE C. WALKER

A Naturalist's Teaching Manual

*Activities and
Ideas for Teaching
Natural History*

Jennifer Bauer Wilson

*Ranger-Naturalist
Tennessee Department of Conservation*

Illustrated by Wynne Brown

A PHalarope Book

PRENTICE HALL PRESS · NEW YORK

Published by Prentice Hall Press
A Division of Simon & Schuster, Inc.

PRENTICE HALL PRESS is a trademark of Simon & Schuster, Inc.

Library of Congress Cataloging-in-Publication Data

Wilson, Jennifer Bauer.
    A naturalist's teaching manual: activities and ideas for teaching
natural history.

    Bibliography
    1. Natural history—Study and teaching.
I. Title.
QH51.W73   1986   508   85-23256
ISBN 0-13-610247-6

Manufactured in the United States of America
10 9 8 7 6 5 4 3 2 1

*For Carrie—may her heart become
one with this marvelous earth!*

Acknowledgments

There are so many to whom acknowledgments are due for their lifelong help in making this book possible by teaching and guiding me to the ways of our environment when I first left the city and came to the mountains.

Thanks go to John Warden, who led me to and taught me everything wonderful about the Southern Appalachian mountains; to all the great folks in the Tennessee state parks who first introduced me to interpretation and gave me the opportunity to share it with others; and to the many children, adults, families, and classrooms who have so openly and eagerly participated in these activities over the years, and have in turn given me new insights into the world around me.

A special thanks to my husband, Jake, for his love, patience, and support: without his initial inspiration I might never have undertaken this book; to my parents for their love and encouragement; and to Carrie, whose charming smile and twinkling eyes always kept me going.

I would also like to thank John Bryant for letting me print his excellent photographs.

Contents

Foreword

The importance of education in a natural setting is too often overlooked by curriculum planners. Many consider it an educational "frill" that does not fit in with the recent "back to basics" educational movement.

Such planners have made a grave mistake. There is nothing frivolous in educating the young about the natural world. Teddy Roosevelt said: "It is safe to say that the prosperity of our people depends directly on the energy and intelligence with which our natural resources are used. It is equally clear that these resources are the final basis of national power and perpetuity."

Roosevelt's words are more true today than they were during his tenure as president. Naturalists, whether in the classroom or park, or speaking before a garden club, have the opportunity to help assure and perpetuate our freedom. Failure to educate a generation about the conservation ethic moves us another step closer to doing ourselves in.

However, if we enlighten every generation to the importance of the earth around and beneath us and strengthen in them the importance of the conservation ethic, our nation will remain strong.

As Americans, we think we're rich because we're smart. But if our earth were a granite ball, we'd be neither rich, nor smart, nor here. Native Americans understood well our temporary tenancy on the earth and recognized the need to live in harmony with the world around them. Today both young and old have an opportunity to gain insight into such a relationship through the teachings of a capable naturalist.

Few understand the critical connection that exists between our natural and developed environments. My credo is: "Our wise continued use of the developed environment offers opportunity for the wise continued use of the natural environment. Our forebears endow us with the developed—we borrow the natural from our children."

To assure adequate resources for the future is our trust for today. The recognition of shared ownership with future generations, or intergenerational equity, is news to millions of folks who haven't thought about it. (Just as they haven't thought about another tongue-twisting term, intertemporal fairness, which relates to fairness across time to future generations.)

This new jargon is not really important to the beginning student and may not be to the instructor. The *ideas* behind the jargon are important. We must curb our selfish and wasteful ways and begin to think about the quality of life for the generations to come.

Because the world faces an uncertain future, many see no need for conservation. But to say that the future is uncertain is to say only that—no more, no less. Just because we're unsure of the future does not relieve us of the responsibility to plan, save, and secure our world for generations not known to us.

Naturalists play an important role in the development of a sense of responsibility toward the earth. They lead people through the process of understanding the world around them by touching a leaf, identifying a bird or its call, or watching and waiting for the creatures of the night. These are often the beginnings of a sense of reverence and awe toward the natural world that is an essential element of a deep concern for the environment.

Jennifer Bauer Wilson is one of the most talented naturalists working in the field today. She's a noted lecturer, writer, group leader, and player of the hammer dulcimer. In this book, she successfully illustrates proven techniques for illuminating things natural.

Charles A. Howell III
Commissioner of Conservation
State of Tennessee

Preface

So often it seems as though the seasons have flown by: Maybe spring passed so quickly that there was not enough time to get out and enjoy the fragrance of wildflowers; or the winter snows suddenly melted away, and not a single snowman was built. As time goes on, so do nature's ways, beckoning us to reach out, slow down a little, and take the time to love and appreciate her wonders.

Within *A Naturalist's Teaching Manual: Activities and Ideas for Teaching Natural History to All Ages*, you will find a selection of outdoor and indoor activities designed for anyone—anywhere—to better acquaint us with the heart of our mother earth.

You may find yourself discovering the tiniest of nature's creatures during an adventure to the outdoors, or exploring nature's wonders indoors in your homes or schools when an outdoor excursion is not possible.

My goal has been to design a book for the young of all ages. Thus, *A Naturalist's Teaching Manual* encompasses crafts, games, discovery trips, art projects, imaginative and creative endeavors, notebooks, experiments, and other ideas to guide the amateur and professional naturalist alike in new and exciting ways to explore our natural world.

Chapter 1
Why a Naturalist?

There's one good thing about going to the mountains in July—getting there!

It had been a long, hot drive through town. The traffic was heavy, the red lights long, and it seemed as though the reflection of that burning sun on the asphalt could cook a body in two seconds flat.

Yet with a little patience and perseverance, the roads soon began to wind and slowly climb. As I passed each rippling creek I could sense the air getting cooler and more fragrant. The soft odor of the damp ground filled me with a sense of oneness with the creations around me. Peeking up beneath the trees, the tiniest of white and violet wildflowers were reaching out their tiny leaves, welcoming in the new day. Here and there a brightly colored bird would flit by, only to be followed by a rustle of branches as a chipmunk scurried back into the leaves.

Not wanting to pass all this by, I pulled over to the side of the road for a moment to absorb this great flurry of activity. For a brief second I thought my heart was going to beat right out of my chest, echoing deep within my body; when up flew a ruffed grouse, startled out of his resting place by my presence. It was sure to be a marvelous day!

"Why do you want to be a naturalist?" folks would ask. There are many other, more lucrative professions. Yet isn't everyone a naturalist at heart? Somewhere deep inside our souls each and every one of us at some time has delighted at the wonders of Mother Nature's creations. It could have been a soft, rumbling summer thundershower; a brilliant rainbow at the end of a storm; or the surprise of seeing a doe dash in front of your car as you rode down the road.

The thrill of the outdoors is something that reaches us all at some time. Even lying out on a rock by a creek in the warm sun is a special treat taken for granted by many, yet too often missed by others who live miles from such lovely places.

Maybe that is when the delight of being a naturalist touches one most strongly. There is nothing more fulfilling than to reach someone's heart and see his or her face light up at the discovery of some new emergence of nature— to see the spider spin its web, or smell the nectar of newly blooming flowers.

Each and every one of us has the ability to awaken another's life to the beauties of the earth's creations. All it takes is a little caring and love for our fragile, ever-changing environment.

There is a very special satisfaction in sharing your love of the wild with others. At times you may feel that no one cares but you, yet the moment you see another's eyes brighten at a newfound discovery, you know your efforts are not all in vain.

I will never forget one special little fellow I met while working for a summer at a Tennessee state park. Throughout the day I would schedule activities for the folks visiting the park. During this particular summer there was one fourteen-year-old boy who joined me for at least half of the programs. We became well acquainted as the weeks

The quiet, changing moods of the outdoors become so apparent as you travel from town to country. Peering across a lake at sunset, you can almost hear the silence, yet know a myriad of life is active all around you. (Photo by John Bryant)

rolled on, and time and time again found ourselves talking about how fascinating were the ways of the American Indian who had at one time occupied the valleys around us.

One thing my friend had always wanted was to find just one real Indian arrowhead. We would walk together in the plowed fields, and though he never gave up, we couldn't seem to find a thing.

It wasn't long before summer was drawing to a close and my young friend was leaving to go back to school. I remembered a few arrowheads at home I had found years ago and thought I would take him one before he left, since our summer hunting luck was not so good.

He was just leaving when I caught up with him and placed that small black piece of artwork in his hand. I only

The colorful runways are quite obvious to an insect searching for the delicious nectar of a flower. Crawl in for a closeup of these sometimes overlooked details.

wish I could describe the look on his face—that's when I knew it was all worthwhile!

It would be a shame to think that anyone could be content with a world of shopping centers, high rises, and concrete, without wild places to refresh our souls and lighten our minds. Yet sharing your concern and care for our natural world with your friends and children may inspire them to learn to love the wild things in life that are so quickly disappearing.

You may wish to be a naturalist on a public basis and work with large groups; a teacher with a class full of eager young minds; on an outing with a group of friends; or a mother or father sharing the ways of the forest with your children.

No matter which group you fall into, you will find within this book ideas, activities, and, hopefully, inspirations that will help to open up the world of nature to you and those with whom you wish to share these ideas. These activities may serve as a catalyst—a catalyst to spark the minds of those you guide.

There is but one very special ingredient you as an individual will need to supply: Sharing your love and enthusiasm for our natural world with those you encounter will be indispensable to you in guiding your friends, family, and acquaintances to the miraculous beauties of our earth!

Chapter 2
A World of Discoveries

Against the window pane I noticed the print of a tiny face, which not long before had peered in wonder at the gentle, new-fallen snow. Across the yard could be seen the track of a small bird hopping joyously through the covered grass. It seemed such a miracle realizing that until today these young eyes had not been blessed with a spectacle as beautiful as a winter snow.

Every part of our world seemingly has a pattern—a goal that each living thing is striving toward. In discovering the outdoors and working as naturalists for our own personal enlightenment or as guides to others, questions arise as to who we might work with, what natural elements we might draw from, and how we begin to approach this new world.

The factors that limit you are your own desires. Your interest as a naturalist may be your personal desire to become more in touch with the world around you. On the other hand, one might prefer to share a love of the out doors with larger groups, such as school classes, visitors to parks and recreational areas, clubs, and other organi-

Nothing can compare to the thrill of discovering something new. A winter snow can be as amazing to an adult as it is to a young child seeing it for the first time.

zations. Anyone, anywhere may come to you to share their excitement in the outdoors—from the tiniest child with eyes peering in amazement at a passing butterfly to the young of all ages.

It doesn't matter where you live—be it the city or the country—the hand of Mother Nature is always there. On a clear day clouds still pass over the cities and grass grows between the sidewalks. You may not feel it is the same as going to the country, but if you look closely you'll find nature at work everywhere. Birds live in towns as well as in the country, trying to survive what we consider environmental development. In the same light, as a naturalist you need to work *with* your resources, not against them.

Admiring the delicacy of a flower is one thing, breaking it off is another. Working "with" a flower would mean leaving it for others to enjoy, letting it flourish and seed to produce offspring.

Virtually everything that exists in this universe can be discovered and enjoyed by those wanting to explore nature. The wonders of the smallest insects working beneath the ground and the enormity of our solar system are all fair game to one who is interested and who cares. If you chose to devote your entire life to leading others to different natural discoveries, the extent of your sources and elements would be never-ending. The real joy is knowing that there will always be something new to discover.

We would never be able to delve into the natural history of every plant, animal, insect, or drop of water in this one book. As your interest blossoms in the myriad of different fields of nature study, you will find there are many books and field guides available to help you become better acquainted with the many varied and special subjects.

How you come across to others and to yourself is one of the most important factors in determining your success as a nature guide. If *you* don't really care, your attitude will be passed on to those you talk with, and they will share the same feelings. On the other hand, your excitement can be just as contagious. The thrill of seeing a doe bound across the road for the very first time—the delight as your heart pounded and you exclaimed "Oh look!"— can be shared with all of those you guide to the world of nature. You needn't be spotting something as dramatic as a doe—the new bloom of a spring lily or the approach of a summer storm can be just as rewarding if you communicate to others that same thrill of discovery.

It is not essential to be right at the heart of our natural world to become a part of it or to introduce folks to it. It would be ideal to be able to step out your back door and have in your grasp every element of the outdoors necessary to study whatever you desire that day. Yet that is not always possible, as so many of us know. We must live and work near towns and cities, attend schools, and take part in daily activities that do not involve a trip to the woods or seashore.

This is absolutely no reason to be discouraged, though. Within our minds is the ability to bring the spirit of nature to our towns, schools, and homes. Look out your window and you're sure to see birds, grass, trees, and a bounty of life at its best. As you proceed through this book, you will find a host of activities that will enchance nature study both indoors and out, and in the city as well as the country.

Through indoor activities you can create a knowledgeable, caring attitude toward the outdoors that can only be enhanced by a firsthand experience of going right to the source of your studies.

After passing the winter months in the classroom or engaging in indoor study at home, it is always nice to plan an outdoor excursion to a special place that intrigues you. Plan a camping trip or pack a lunch for a day hike in one

Nature's spirit can be found from the towering limbs of an elderly oak tree to the finely spun threads of the web of this early riser.

of your nearby parks; or maybe a trip to the seashore would be more to your liking. Whatever your preference is, the hands-on experience will be exciting for you and those you work with.

Working as a naturalist in a state park over the course of one summer, I met so many wonderful people. It was as though just being there lightened and opened the spirits of those who journeyed to the outdoors, to the wonders of what a special place nature's domain really can be. It is in the parks that you meet so many folks who are away from schools and towns for their vacations, executing the plans for an outdoor excursion that they have waited so long for.

Your efforts as a nature guide will truly be heightened as you see the thrill of finding new wonders in the outdoors touch those who share their newfound excitement with you. That excitement was especially meaningful to an eight-year-old named Brian who joined me on a summer hike one day in a state park. A group of about twelve of us were going out along a trail around the lake. We carried with us a few large garbage bags as we walked, hoping to clean up the litter around the lake shore. As we strolled down the trail, enjoying the melodies of the rippling water, we discussed the subject of litter—what it was, where it went, and what we could do about it. Everyone in the group was helping to clean the trail, including Brian. He hung on tight to his litter bag, filling it only with what he found. He even managed to get the remains of an old rubber raft in his bag! Pretty soon his bag was so full that it was larger than him, yet he managed to drag it on alone, not wanting anyone to help him carry it.

When we reached the end of the trail we walked up to the trash cans, where everyone deposited their litter bags—that is, everyone but Brian. He had decided to keep his just a little bit longer: just long enough to carry it around the entire campground and show everyone all the litter he had so proudly helped to clean up!

It is your enthusiasm that will make your efforts to reach others a success. If Brian's guide had not really cared whether the litter was there or not, then Brian probably

Take the time to share your love of our natural world with your friends, family, and all you become acquainted with—your excitement will surely be contagious.

wouldn't have cared either. The fact that you are interested and excited about what you are sharing with others can only stimulate that same excitement in your friends, children, and family. Never let that thrill of discovery and rediscovery die, and in turn the thrill of seeing life renewed will continually open its arms to you!

Chapter 3
Introductory Activities to Awaken the Senses

If you were to stand in a quiet spot deep within the mountain forest and listen and look very intently, all the different forms of life one could observe scurrying in every direction could easily be overwhelming. To be aware of so much in such a busy world sometimes takes a specially trained ear and heart.

It is so easy to miss many of the activities around us. In our everyday, workaday lives we find ourselves running at such a fast pace: keeping time with the clock, making meetings, or rushing to the store. At the same time, our daily surroundings often do not provide us with the most aesthetic environment. As each day comes and goes, so many of us spend our daily routines in situations that are not sensually pleasing.

Stop for a moment and think of the things you encounter on a regular basis. Do any of these things ring a bell? Heavy traffic, honking horns, car exhaust, factory emissions, folks pushing their way through crowds, loud noises, slamming doors, just to name a few.

Add to this an overabundance of buildings, shopping centers, and concrete, and then subtract most of the trees

Open all of your senses to the world around you. As you find your way to new, inspirational places, their sounds, fragrances, and feelings will remain in your memory, lightening your spirit on those days when you cannot travel. (Photo by John Bryant)

and vegetation that once grew in their place, and you have painted all or part of a very familiar scene.

The effect on our perceptual abilities is often subtle and could go unnoticed. Even when we enter the realm of the great outdoors, we sometimes miss its special ways or messages.

Yet how could we possibly miss something as wonderful as nature itself when we have in fact gone to it to take a break from city life?

It is sometimes easy to "turn off" our senses to our surroundings when we find them undesirable or offensive. In order to deal with excessive noise, it may be necessary to close our ears to it. When we see the same scene every day, we tend to stop looking and let it just pass by.

In returning to our mother earth we need to slow down, relax, and take the time to reawaken our five senses to the softness and beauty of our natural world.

"Sense-awakening" activities can be done indoors or outdoors, with young or old, with families, in classrooms, or individually; the results are still the same—a pathway to a whole new realm of discoveries!

The following activities are designed to reawaken senses that have sometimes been slightly dulled by the harshness of everyday life. The focus of each activity will be on one particular sense, with the possible exception of sight. Of course, do not omit the other activities if they can be beneficial.

For instance, in the first activity you will notice that "touch" is the main focus, yet with particular types of leaves smell could also be used to make their identity more memorable. The only senses you would not want to use are sight and taste: Sight would detract from the point of the activity, and taste could be dangerous since many leaves can be poisonous if ingested.

Before beginning any of these activities with your

group, take a few minutes to discuss with them the reasons why they are doing this. Emphasize that it can be fun! If this is understood before you begin, you will find a more receptive audience, and a much better learning situation created at the onset of the activities.

ONE SPECIAL LEAF

WHICH SENSE: Touch

IDEAL LOCATION: a. Have your group find a quiet, soft spot in the forest, or

b. Leaves can be collected and brought indoors.

BEST GROUP SIZE: 10–20

Feel each vein, outline every edge, smell the fragrance of your special leaf, for when you lay it back down, you will know it like a friend.

First have your group situated in a comfortable position, preferably in a circle. If you are in the woods, clear a space in the center of the circle so the leaves you have picked up won't mix with the rest of the forest floor. (Always remember to return the woods to their natural appearance before you leave!)

Each person is asked to close his or her eyes (you can use the honor system or blindfolds if you wish), and then you give each person in the circle one leaf that is their "special leaf." While they have their eyes closed, encourage them to trace every vein and outline the edges with their fingers. They are to become so acquainted with "their" leaf through the sense of touch that when you take back all the leaves and mix them up in the center of the circle, each person should be able to find his or her "special leaf" amidst the leaves in the pile!

RECALL

WHICH SENSE: Sight (with emphasis on noticing the details of nature and sharpening our abilities to observe the many things we so easily miss on a walk through the woods)

IDEAL LOCATION: Good for a little indoor mind exercise

BEST GROUP SIZE: 1–100

Prior to beginning you will need to do a little "artwork" in preparation. This doesn't need to be fancy, just easy for folks sitting at a distance to distinguish. Get a piece of poster board and draw a cartoon-like picture of a woodland scene. For instance, a tree, an owl on a limb, a swing from a branch with a spider wearing tennis shoes on the swing, two or three rainclouds, six drops of water coming from the cloud, and so on. After you have finished your drawing, go back and compose ten to twenty questions relating to the picture. Questions like "How many raindrops are coming out of the cloud?" "What was on the spider's feet?" or "How many legs did the spider have?" are good examples. Let your imagination run wild with this—preparing it is half the fun. When you are with your group, explain to them that you are going to let them look at a picture for one minute, and after you turn the picture upside down they are to answer a set number of questions.

You might want to throw out a few hints about the details of the questions so they are not taken totally by surprise. By getting a feel for how many details each person missed, you can emphasize how this little game acted as a personal test for each person, giving each one an idea of just how observant or unobservant he or she is.

MY SPECIAL PLACE

WHICH SENSE: Sight, touch, smell, hearing

IDEAL LOCATION: Outdoors provides a more inspiring atmosphere, but in a classroom this will work just as well.

BEST GROUP SIZE: 10–30

Relax your group by discussing feelings and experiences that are pleasing when spending time outdoors or in the

Your special place may be under a tree in your back yard or on a rock by a singing creek. Wherever this spot may be, it will be special because it is yours.

woods. Once the mood is created it will be much easier for the group to let their imaginations go and vividly describe their "special place."

Ask each person to quietly recreate in their mind a very special place that stands out in their memory.

Once they have an image of this place in mind, ask them to think of ten words (descriptive) that would create an image of the place for the rest of the group, yet wouldn't tell what the place is; for instance, "warm," "shady," "earthy," "sturdy," and so on. Each person should write down the ten words on a piece of paper, put their name on it, and fold it up. Collect all the papers and have each person draw one out of a bowl. Each person would read the ten words they drew to the group, and the group in turn then tries to guess what this "special place" is.

OUT OF SIGHT!

WHICH SENSE: Touch

IDEAL LOCATION: Anywhere!

BEST GROUP SIZE: 2–100

This can be quite a fun activity as there is always a sense of mystery as to what is hidden from your sight. You will need to do a little preparation by collecting things in the woods and fields. For instance, a pine cone, a stick, a small rock, a leaf, or whatever your imagination and eyes can find that would be fun to use. Just be sure to get only things that are not in a living or growing state! (There's no need to destroy things unncecessarily.) You'll be able to find plenty of interesting things lying on the forest floor.

Next you will need several brown lunch bags. Place an object in each bag and fold the top down. You are now ready to begin.

You will ask one member of your group to reach down in the bag without looking and feel what is in there. There are many things that they will recognize right away . . . but you must stress that they cannot blurt out what it is!

The idea of the game is for the person feeling the object to describe it without saying what it is so that the rest of the group can try to guess it.

You may need to stress the idea that the person feeling should forget what the object looks like and should just concentrate on how it feels (rough or smooth, long or short, soft or hard). We can become so dependent on our sense of sight that it can be difficult at first to completely block it out and depend solely on touch, but with a little persuasion it can be done.

Whoever guesses what is in the bag gets to feel the second hidden object. If the describer and feeler are successful in getting someone to guess what they are feeling, they have done an excellent job of tuning in to their sense of touch.

A SNIFF-AND-FEEL HIKE

WHICH SENSE: Smell

IDEAL LOCATION: Outdoors, definitely!

BEST GROUP SIZE: Approximately 10

In our everyday, rushing life-styles we tend to fly by a lot, especially all the beautiful odors and textures of the outdoors and the woods. In this activity we will slow down to a crawl, investigating each and every little life form growing beneath our feet or towering above our heads.

The title of the activity tells us what we will be doing. With your group, head out into the forest, taking the time to feel gently the small hairs on a leaf, or sniff the luscious odor of the bark of a wild cherry. Get down on your hands and knees and feel the soft texture of the soil; smell its rich, earthy tones.

As you are discovering all these details of the outdoors, take the time to have the group discuss how these new odors and feelings affect them. This activity combines very well with "My Special Place." Using the same idea, you can have each person describe in the same way something they felt or some odor they liked so the group can guess what it is and remember how special it was themselves.

Don't let the enormity of a spot overwhelm you, for within its chasms are textures and odors that will give this place its own personality. Let the water spill over your hands, smell the dampness of the soil, and gently run your fingers over the outlines of fossils within the rocks as you learn a new place on your sniff and feel hike.

JUST YOU AND ME

WHICH SENSE: Touch, smell, and sound

IDEAL LOCATION: Outdoors—a combination of field and forest works nicely.

BEST GROUP SIZE: Any number, as long as each person has a partner.

By turning off your sense of sight, you can more easily open up your remaining senses and experience the wonders of our world magnified to an exceptional degree. In each pair, one person closes his or her eyes or is blindfolded. The other person is the leader, as he or she will be guiding the blindfolded partner around. The one who can see has the job of taking the partner to different things that will enhance their senses. Have them feel the bark of a tree from the ground up, feel the coolness of the water and the texture of the bottom silt, smell the blooming of a rose, or listen to the sounds of a coming storm. Each little thing will seem amazingly vivid; as you cannot see it, you will find yourself tuning in to the life around you much more easily and missing very little of it!

Even the tiniest of things are fair game as you guide your blindfolded partner along the way as "Just You and Me" explore the world around us.

Remember, if you are the leader you need to tell your partner where to step, when to duck, and protect him or her from any unseen hazards. That's what makes this such a special walk.

After one person had had a turn being blindfolded, change positions so each of you can experience the sensation of opening up your senses to the world!

A SILENT TIME

WHICH SENSE: All

IDEAL LOCATION: A quiet place in the woods, near a stream or lake, or wherever you feel you can relax and let your senses go!

BEST GROUP SIZE: Can be any number of people, but the activity is done individually.

After experiencing all or part of the previous activities, this is a pleasant exercise to do to gather your thoughts and feelings.

You might remember your special place when you try to decide on an ideal location for you to spend your quiet time. Wherever you may choose, find yourself a quiet, comfortable spot, sit down, and relax completely.

Now is the time to open up all of your senses to life around you. Ours is such a marvelous world, and by this point you should be aware of the many tiny, sometimes unnoticed goings-on around you.

During your quiet time, close out anything unpleasant to you and just absorb the lovely sounds, sights, odors, and textures around you. If you are with a group, you might set a time limit as to how long everyone is out on their own, possibly spending several hours enjoying the wonders of nature.

Make the best of this special time. You will find yourself much more relaxed and open to life around you!

Chapter 4
Start Small: Looking for the Little Things

As we step through the woods, beneath our feet lie many small, yet very significant things. Their minute size sometimes causes them to be overlooked, even though they may be just as special and colorful as their larger counterparts.

There is something out there that gives nature its color and character, and it is probably all those little things piled together that paint the picture we see when we gaze into the out-of-doors.

A DECAYING LOG—NATURE'S SPECIAL PLACE

Becoming acquainted with a downed tree or log can show you many parts of nature's realm. Take along your sketchbook as you explore these tiny details so you can record your findings of this little city, much like discovering a lost place such as Atlantis.

Every decaying log is different, so the wonders will frequently change as you find new things at which to look.

What is growing on the surface of the log? If you look closely you might discover patches of flat, blue-green plants spreading across the surface. Some of them may have protrusions growing out of them, but they will all take on that characteristic blue-green color. These are lichens, a very unusual plant in that it is composed of not one, but two types of plants—one a fungus, the other an algae. In order for a lichen to grown and thrive, it first needs clean, unpolluted air, but if this requirement is met they can be found in abundance.

You may also find growing on the log different types of mushrooms of all colors, shapes, and sizes. Mosses, growing long and compact against the log, may spread a deep green across the surface along with seedlings of trees, shrubs, and herbs that have found the log a perfect habitat to germinate and begin their new life.

Not only might you find different colors and forms of plants, but there will also be insects of the most interesting kinds living within the log. A field guide to insects would be helpful in identifying what you see, but your sketchbook will prove indispensable in saving you the burden of having to carry a library out into the field. When you return from your trek, look at the sketches you made of the life on the log. If you want to find out more about what you have found, now is the time to refer to a guide or two to zero in on the special characteristics of what you have discovered.

The next time you step over a fallen log, remember—this is not just a chunk of wood lying on the ground, but a very special part of the forest, returning all the energy it gathered during its lifetime back to the ground. It is this energy that is helping all the things thrive and grow that you discovered on your special log.

CAMOUFLAGE IN NATURE

It is quite amazing how well all the living things in the forest can blend together. The overall appearance is of a mass of color and shape, yet if you break it down you will find a wealth of insects, birds, animals, and plants, resting on the sides of trees and limbs; all blending so well that it sometimes takes a sharp eye to pick them out.

Here is a little game that will help sharpen the eye and imagination to get you ready for spotting the finer things in the outdoors.

Searching for our hidden objects will be very similar to an Easter egg hunt. There should be at least two people involved in this activity, but the more the merrier. At least one person will be in charge of hiding different-colored pipe cleaners along a given stretch of trail or field. The people doing the hiding need to tie the pipe cleaners in areas that are obvious, yet where their color will blend with what you have tied them to. Don't stick a pipe cleaner under a rock, for instance, for it will never be found. They need to be right out in the open, and if they are tied to things they blend well with, they will still be difficult to spot. You might want to tie some of the pipe cleaners together in the shapes of animals and stick figures to give them more realistic forms.

When the trail is stocked with pipe-cleaner creatures,

the rest of the group will go along the same path and see if they can find where all these creatures are sitting. As your eyes become conditioned to what you are looking for, it will become a little easier.

Nature has blended its creatures with their environment in the same manner to help protect them and aid in ensuring their survival. Now that you are well practiced in finding your pipe-cleaner creatures, you will soon become a real pro at finding the many living things that are blending in much the same way all around us!

MICROHABITATS

Exploring the world of the little guys is the idea behind microhabitats. This is an activity for one to one hundred, working exceptionally well with small teams of two to five. Each team is given a pencil and pad of paper and sent out on a journey to explore a particular microhabitat. They may be sent to a bank beside a creek, a flat area in a field, or a rocky spot in the woods. Any area will work just fine; the idea is to become thoroughly acquainted with the habitat that has been assigned to each team.

Each team should appoint a secretary, who will take notes and record all the team's observations. As you explore your area, list absolutely everything that is there, even down to the holes in the leaves and the bark chips from the tree above.

After each team returns with its description, have the secretary read to all the teams what each team has found; then, as a large group, discuss just what all these discoveries mean to the ways of our natural world. Why are there holes in the leaf? What made the bark fall to the ground? Are there insects living under the bark?

You will find that each and every thing listed by each team can open up the door to a whole new world beneath our feet.

When the discussion is over, each team member might like to draw a picture of the most outstanding elements of the microhabitat they studied as a remembrance of the tinier things in nature.

A PEEPER PARTY

One of my favorite sounds of spring is the mysterious, high-pitched chorus of "preeps" that seems to arise miraculously from deep within the grass during a warm shower. What could this happy little song be that croons us to sleep by the pond's edge and keeps us company on warm summer evenings?

It is the call of a very tiny tree frog, the spring peeper. Being a small (¾–1⅜-inch) fellow, he is sometimes quite hard to spot. His coloring is a tannish brown, with a dark X on his back. One of the fun things about observing peepers is seeing the round toe pads that aid them in climbing grass blades and the like.

It seems that the spring peeper's singing hours usually occur after dark or in the late evening. To top that off, their size and ability to camouflage their presence make it necessary for a person to have a keen eye to pick them out of their surroundings. But don't let that stop you from having a good look at a very interesting little fellow. By

going on a "peeper hunt" you just might be able to find a spring peeper in full chorus!

When hunting peepers, you will almost feel like an Indian scout or hunter, silently stalking your prey, for you will have to approach the peepers slowly and quietly.

All you will need is a flashlight in your search for the illusive tree frog. To start your hunt, stand very quietly near a pond or area where you can hear the peepers calling. Close your eyes and concentrate on just one voice out of the bunch, preferably the one that sounds closest to you. Look directly at the area where the voice you have chosen is coming from and take very gentle steps in that direction. Now stop . . . is he still singing? If he isn't, stand there silently and he should start up in a moment; if the frog hears you he will stop his call until you are silent again. Once he begins again, take a few more quiet steps in his direction, repeating this process until you are within seeing distance from his perch. More than likely he will be down in the grass, sitting halfway up a blade in full splendor. Shine your flashlight in the spot you have tuned your ears onto and you will probably be rewarded by a great look at the fellow we frequently hear but seldom see!

SPRING SURPRISES

After spring is well under way and the wildflowers are in full bloom, the ferns have unfolded their fronds, and the once-new seedlings are growing rapidly by the day, it is easy to forget that only a few months previously, these flourishing plants were very small and just beginning a new life.

On a warm spring day, nothing is more exciting than going on a search through the fields and forests looking for the faces of our green friends poking up through the ground.

With a group, alone, or with your family, devote a little time on a pretty day to a trek to the outdoors in search of these signs that life is once again renewing itself.

To make the journey a bit challenging, see who has the sharpest eye and can find the most "little" signs of spring. Bring along a pad and paper with the name of each person in the group listed across the top. Draw columns down the page, and have someone keep track of what has been discovered by placing it under the name of the person who found it. This is especially fun with children, as they love to be the first to find something new and will look extra hard for new discoveries.

Everyone should carry their own pad of paper too, so they can sketch the special things they have found, as well as jotting down what they are doing. Give your drawings comical characteristics; make them seem almost human. A mushroom just pushing its way through the ground sometimes keeps a roof over its head, composed of twigs, leaves, and soil, which looks almost like a flat hat.

The tiny uncurling frond of a new fern seems to reach

out its hand to those who pass. As a new leaf unfolds at the end of a tree branch, you can almost see a dancer spinning in motion.

Remember, the spectacle of spring occurs but once a year—don't let it pass you by!

Chapter Five
Think Green: Getting Acquainted with Plants

It is really a miracle that every spring, after the cold snows have melted from beneath our feet, the tiny seeds that have rested in the soil below suddenly poke forth their heads and emerge, growing into new plants, to carry on the coming summer season!

With all this happening beneath the ground, we seem to miss just how and when it all happens, yet there are ways we can view the emergence of a seed.

THE LIFE OF A SEED

A regular garden bean seed works very well for this activity, as it is large and very easy to view. The supplies needed are few: a glass, a piece of blotting paper, water, and of course your seed or seeds.

Cut your blotting paper to a size that will line the curve of the glass and lie flush against the glass on the inside. Fill the glass with water, letting it sit just long enough for the paper to become saturated, then pour out the remaining water, leaving just enough in the bottom (say 1-inch deep) to keep the paper damp. Slide your seeds down between the paper and the glass so you can see them from the outside of the glass.

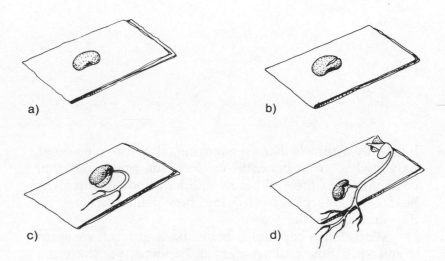

a)

b)

c)

d)

Keeping a notebook or record of the next week's accomplishments will be fun, for every day the seeds will slowly change as you get to watch the germination right before your eyes. Take the time every day to date a page in your notebook and sketch what your seed looks like that day. Jot down any observations you might want to add. For instance, if the root starts out toward the sky, what do you notice happening after a day or two? It will be amazing to watch and record, and at the end have a fascinating day-by-day account of what your seed did. The next time the spring seeds emerge from the ground, you will be able to remember from watching your seed in the glass just what nature has intended for them to do in order to grow!

MEDICINAL PLANTS

There are so many different plants, trees, and shrubs growing across our continent, imagine the job it would be to learn all their identities! Rather than trying to learn them all, choose a smaller group of plants of particular interest to you. Medicinal plants comprise a group that represents a fascinating realm of our past traditions.

The roots, leaves, stems, flowers, and even seeds of some groups of plants have been used in herbal medicines over the centuries to produce liquid remedies, salves, ointments, and the like in efforts to heal the illnesses and discomforts of generations. This concept of herbal healing is not all poppycock either, for it is from many of these remedies that our chemically based drugs have been derived.

There is much we can learn from the old ways of survival, including the use of medicinal plants. The following page contains diagrams of some of the more common plants to be found in this country, along with their uses.

Nowadays it is not a good idea to collect wild plants. In many instances, their numbers are few; it is doubtful they would thrive if they were to be removed from their natural habitats. Leaving them alone offers everyone an opportunity to see them and reflect on the old days when their remedies were the only ways known to help ease illnesses and discomforts.

If you want to pursue the subject further, there are many books and guides on medicinal plants and remedies available in libraries and book stores.

FROM THIS GREEN EARTH: SOME COMMON MEDICINALS

a) Witch Hazel (*Hamamelis virginiana*)
    Healing and astringent for cuts and sprains

b) Honeysuckle (*Lonicera* sp.)
    A juice from the vine will ease bee stings; an extract is said to alleviate asthma and lung problems.

c) White Pine (*Pinus strobus*)
    A remedy from the bark is said to ease a cough and sore throat; an extract from the cone acts as a cure for rheumatism.

d) Jewelweed (*Impatiens biflora*)
    Crushed leaves said to alleviate itch from poison ivy, bee stings and stinging nettle.

e) Elderberry, blue-berried variety (*Sambucus canadensis*)
    Leaf ointment for bruises and sprains; warmed leaves applied to forehead for headache; elder flower water for suppression of freckles and to ease pain from sunburn.

THE WORLD OF GALLS

During some of your plant hunts you might find unusual growths on the leaves and stems of plants. These are called *galls*; they are actually the homes of very tiny insect larvae. An adult female insect lays her egg in the plant, which reacts by producing a swelling and abnormal growth around the egg. This temporary home for the developing insect larvae acts as a shelter and food supply to get the new insect off to a good start.

Galls are interesting to find and identify, for out of the more than 1500 gall-producing insects, it has been found that each particular insect works on only one species of plant.

If you find a gall in the summer, still developing, put it on a thin layer of moist soil in a jar with a screened cover and observe what comes out of the gall when it is fully developed. If you are not sure as to whether something has already emerged, look closely at your gall for any small hole that may have been the exit point for the creature inside. As long as the gall is still solid, its inhabitant is still inside.

TALKING TO THE TREES

Our forests are filled with many lovely trees. On a walk through the woods you can find anything from the tiniest seedling to a tree fifty or more years old. Before the massive clear-cuts of the late 1800s and early 1900s the southeastern forests boasted many large, stately trees well over 100 years old. Today it is rare to find a stand of virgin timber, but on occasion we can find a stump or a log incorporated into a building.

a) Goldenrod ball gall

b) Oak apple gall

c) Woolly gall

d) Maple leaf spot gall

e) Spruce gall

f) Hackberry nipple gall

By counting the number of rings across the surface of a tree stump, a wealth of information can be found about the life of that tree and the climate in which it grew. The rings are a storybook telling the tree's history. If you count the number of rings from the center of a stump on out, the age of the tree can be determined, for each ring indicates one year's growth. The distance between the rings is also a good clue, for the farther apart each ring is, the wetter the season. Rings that are very close indicate a dry spell.

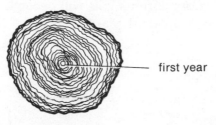

first year

The giant sequoias of our western states are marvels to behold. They are said to have the capability to live up to 5,000 years. The American Museum of Natural History in New York has on exhibit a sequoia that did not get to live out its promised years. It was just a "child" when it died, measuring 16½ feet in diameter inside the bark; its tree rings date it as being 1341 years old!

The shape of tree rings was proven to be an indicator of air pollution back in 1912 along the Ohio River, south of Pittsburgh. Trees with thin, erratic rings; small leaves; and stunted growth were all found in the path of industrial smoke and fumes. Yet just one mile downstream, outside of the pollution, the rings and growth patterns of trees were normal and healthy.

It would be wonderful to know the changes in the forest that have happened around the noble trees that have been standing for 100 years or more. By their rings, those that are no longer alive have left us clues to their age, the climate, and the surroundings of this home to so many creatures.

LEARNING TO KEY

The more you begin to discover on your jaunts to the outdoors, the more curious you will become as to exactly what all these wonderful plants might be. The urge to

a) Birdfoot violet

b) Round leaf yellow violet

c) Bracket fungus

d) Caesar's mushroom

identify can become overwhelming, just as the quantity and variety of life itself are overwhelming!

To get started learning to identify, you might like to try using the following practice plant keys. Professional folks and amateurs alike find using keys the best method of identifying the different plants and animals that they do not know. The keys can be tricky to use if you are not familiar with their basic setup.

These practice keys are designed so anyone can learn the basics of identifying even the most difficult species. The basic idea is to ask the reader two or more questions about the plant or animal in question. When you decide which statement best applies to what you have found, you move on to the next letter or number referred to at the end of the statement you have chosen. By proceeding in this fashion you should arrive at an identification for what you are trying to identify. Proceed through the key that follows, answering each question and then moving on to the letter or number referred to at the end of each step. You should be able to begin identifying plants in this fashion. When you get the hang of it you might like to try a more comprehensive key, which you can find in any field or botanical guide. The answers to each key can be found at the end of each keying section.

Practice Key

Take a close look at the drawings on the preceding page and answer the questions on page 56. Work on one drawing at a time with every answer you pick directing you to another numbered question. (When you come to a dead end this is just an indication that you could continue indefinitely through all of the plants in the plant kingdom if you so desired!) After you have answered the questions correctly you will soon find out the name of the plant in the drawing!

1. Plant with chlorophyll (green) 2
1. Plant without chlorophyll   6

   2. Petals 4 or fewer
   2. Petals 5   3

3. Flowers light in color   4
3. Flowers dark, usually violet 5

   4. Leaves roundish to   Round Leaf Yellow Violet
      heart shaped
   4. Leaves other   5

5. Leaves deeply cut   Birdfoot Violet
5. Leaves oblong

   6. Plant fleshy with gills   7
   6. Plant woody with pores, Bracket fungus
      growing on log

7. Stalk emerging from   Caesar's Mushroom
   saclike cup
7. Stalk arising directly
   from the ground

Chapter Six
Fly High: Making Friends with Birds

What a wonderful life, to be able to fly high in the sky, sail to the ground, and then soar off again. Just imagine all the different sizes and colors of birds that grace the skies of the United States alone! From a large black crow to a tiny, flittering hummingbird, one can find an array of these feathered creatures to delight any imagination.

Glancing toward the heavens, you may see the dark outline of a small songbird or large hawk finding its way past the clouds. If you take some extra time to get to know the birds a little more closely, you will be quite delighted with the discoveries you will make.

The two most important pieces of equipment for studying birds are binoculars and a good field guide complete with color photographs. (I still remember how excited I was when I first discovered that the chestnut-sided warbler was not just a gray spot darting through a rhododendron shrub, but a myriad of color, a natural painting anyone would be proud to display!) With guide and binoculars in hand, you will be more than prepared to try out some of the following activities.

VOICES OF BIRDS—HOW TO LEARN THEM

Identifying a bird by its song, never seeing it, but only hearing its sweet melodies in the woods? Surely I must be kidding! It can be done, and it is one of the most fascinating and rewarding pastimes in studying birds.

You need to be patient, for it takes a little time to adjust your ears to the songs of the birds, but once you tune in, you'll never be able to tune out.

Find yourself a quiet spot where you won't be disturbed by the sounds of traffic or other distractions. Listen for the sounds around you. To learn a bird song, it will be helpful to attach words, sentences, phrases, and phonetic patterns to the sounds you are hearing. By association, those phrases will become familiar to you whenever you hear a certain species singing. This is an age-old art, as birdwatchers over the years have used this practice in remembering the songs of birds. Below are some of the phrases used for a few more common birds.

Birds that say their name:
COMMON FLICKER—"flicka flicka flicka"
EASTERN PEEWEE—"pee-a-wee" (slurring up), "pee-ur" (slurring down)
GRAY CATBIRD—mews like a cat
WHIPPOORWILL—"whip poor weel" (repeated)
Birds of field and forest:
TUFTED TITMOUSE—"peter peter peter" (chanting)
CAROLINA WREN—"tea ket'tle tea ket'tle"
EASTERN MEADOWLARK—"spring is here" (quavering last note)
NORTHERN CARDINAL—"cheer cheer cheer"
WOOD THRUSH—"ee-oo-lay" (flutelike, holding last note)
RUFOUS-SIDED TOWHEE—"drink your teeee" (holding last note)

A few warblers:
YELLOW WARBLER—"sweet, sweet, sweet, I'm so sweet" (rapid and cheery)
COMMON YELLOWTHROAT—"witchity, witchity, witch" (bouncy)
OVENBIRD—"teach, teach, teach" (becoming progressively louder)
A couple of nighttime visitors:
SCREECH OWL—mournful, trembling wail
BARRED OWL—"Who cooks for you? Who cooks for you all?" (last note drops off)

If you are teaching yourself, try to identify the bird by sight first, then listen until the words and patterns you have attached to its melody repeat over and over in your mind. Any good field guide to birds will give you a description of the voice of each species, along with sounds and phonetics to make it more easily recognizable. Going into the field with someone who already knows a few bird songs is the easiest way to get started, but if this isn't possible, you'll be able to teach yourself by fine-tuning your ears and eyes.

MUSIC TO YOUR EARS

Another way to become acquainted with the many different bird songs is by listening to one of the excellent records available that denote each species with an example of their song.

To make learning bird songs even more exciting, try this little game of bird music. Everyone participating will first need to listen to certain chosen species of birds on a record. (These records are available in some local libraries, university libraries, and book stores. Please see Bibliography for sources.) You may want to choose ten agreed-upon species for everyone to become familiar with. After all members of the group feel comfortable with their newly learned songs, a leader should be chosen to begin the game.

You might consider this "multiple-choice bird music," because you will have some choices to make. The leader will tell the players that they are about to hear the song of a certain bird—for instance, a chickadee. He will play three songs; the players will try to guess which one of the three is the chickadee. Have them write down their answers so at the end of the game you can go back and see how everyone is doing. In doing this with children, it is always fun to throw in something silly—for instance, telling them to pick out the song of a robin and then playing something like the cry of the screech owl.

After a few rounds of this game you will be quite ready to head to the outdoors to listen to the real bird in action.

ATTRACTING HUMMINGBIRDS

As each warm spring day comes and goes, you'll begin to notice the arrival of more and more migratory birds. One of the most interesting ones to visit the garden is the little hummingbird.

The hummingbird is quite a marvelous creature, rotating its wings at 60–90 revolutions per minute, enabling it to hover in one place. Its brilliant color and rapid movements make it quite a joy to see as the summer approaches.

The hummingbird feeds on the nectar of blooming plants, preferring red, tubular flowers. At times it may take advantage of sapsucker borings, which enable them to enjoy the sugar maple, apple, or willow sap. As they fly from flower to flower they carry the pollen on their bill and forehead, helping to cross-pollinate the flowers.

Their nests, tiny in size, are constructed of the down from willow, milkweed, thistle, or cinnamon fern.

If you've ever thought of trying to attract hummingbirds to your garden, you might try the following ideas: To bring them in early and possibly encourage nesting, you might plant shrubs such as sweet azalea or lilac. Flowers that the hummingbird seems to enjoy includes iris, columbine, sweet william, and phlox. Following the early bloomers, try basswood, weigela, cottoneaster, blueberry, New Jersey tea, trumpet creeper vine, honeysuckle, or morning glory. Other flowers to consider are the beebalm, cardinal flower, four o'clock, foxglove, fuchsia, gladiolus, hollyhock, lily, mint, petunia, scarlet sage, snapdragon, and Virginia bluebell.

In addition to blooming plants, folks have had great success with hummingbird feeders. You can purchase special containers designed for these birds with long narrow feeders or tubes, or you may use plastic or glass vials or test tubes. These should be filled with one part sugar mixed with two to three parts water, and hung from a tree or porch. Allowing a few dead limbs to remain on the tree you hang it from will provide a perching spot and possibly allow you a closer look. Also, adding a little red food coloring to your water mixture will give the impression of that bright red flower the hummingbird so enjoys.

Once you have everything ready, just sit back, and

with a little luck you might find your home visited by a very special little bird.

MAKING A PINE CONE BIRD FEEDER

This is an easy yet effective way to bring several small songbirds in for a closer look with very few, inexpensive materials.

The first thing you will need to do is go out and borrow one pine cone for each feeder from the forest floor. (When we are through with our feeders, what could be better than to return the cones to the woods so they can continue decaying and resupplying the ground with its energy?)

From the end of each cone, tie a string long enough to hang it from a tree branch. Then, in the spaces between each pine cone bract, stuff a little bit of peanut butter.

Now all you need to do is hang your pine cone from a branch in your yard and the birds will soon find this new feast—and you'll be able to watch to see who comes to visit.

SHAPES AND FORMS

You're not always going to be able to get nose to nose with a bird. Sometimes their silhouette against the sky will be the only appearance before they fly off. As a help in recognizing the shapes and forms of a few birds, you will find below a short guide to some of the more common ones you may encounter.

a) Hawk   b) Vulture   c) Owl

d) Song sparrow   e) Meadowlark

f) Mourning dove   g) Barn swallow

h) Blue jay   i) Cardinal

Chapter 7
Get Wet: Discovering the World of Water and Pond Life

On a hot summer day, what could be a better way to introduce yourself to the life and ways of the creeks, rivers, branches, and even ponds, than by going out there and getting your feet wet!

From a short distance away, a rambling creek appears to be a tumbling flow of rushing water passing over rocks and logs. What we don't see is the enormous quantity of life that has made the water their home.

WATER RAMBLE—GETTING YOUR FEET WET

A firsthand way to discover who and what is living beneath the currents is to become a part of the water ourselves. This is a shallow-water activity, though—please do not go venturing out in water much past your ankles, for the shallow areas are all you will need to discover water life.

It is in the ankle-deep water that you will have better views of activity on the bottom; there you will be able to

a) Green frog (*Rana clamitans*).

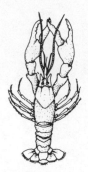

c) Red eft or Red-spotted newt
(*Notopthalmus viridescens*).

b) Crayfish (after Pennak).

d) Alligator snapping turtle
(*Macroclemys temminckii*).

e) Water strider (*Gerris* sp.)
(after Pennak).

f) Whirligig beetle(*Dineutus*
sp.).

g) Dragonfly nymph (*Macromia
magnifica*) (*after Pennak*).

h) Snail shell.

i) Caddis fly larval house
("*stickbait*").

touch a few things and then return them to their homes.

In wading out into the creeks and streams, you need to venture out very gently, making as few waves as possible. The more you disturb the water the less you will be able to see, so move slowly and carefully. You will see the most if you stop frequently and scan the area around you. Your constant motion works against the constant motion of the water, so you will have to depend on your ability to stand quietly.

As you look for water life, check the bottoms of rocks for small larvae hanging on; in little holes and under rocks, crawdads will be sitting in wait for dinner to venture by; small snails may be hanging onto the larger rocks; and water striders may be seen darting across the surface of the water. Those are only a few of the things to be viewed. Following is a guide that will help you recognize some of the more common creatures you may find on your water ramble. These are creatures truly worthy of admiration, spending their lifetime attached to rocks, in holes, living a life that is constantly moving with and sometimes against the strong currents of the ever-flowing waters. Living within the water is a way of life very different from our own, yet also similar, as it reflects all creatures' instincts to survive.

HAY INFUSION STUDIES

On our water ramble we discovered some of the interesting creatures that are visible to the eye, things we could see at our feet. Yet think of all the life teeming in our waters that we cannot see. These are forms of life so tiny that some can just barely be seen swimming with the naked eye—and some can be seen only with the aid of a microscope!

To do a hay infusion study, a microscope would be quite helpful. If one is not available, there are still several things you can see with your eye or with the aid of a hand lens. This project may seem very similar to keeping a fish aquarium, with the exception that this study only lasts two or three weeks before you need to return the water life to the pond or creek.

To start, you will need a one-gallon glass jar or something similar, possibly a fishbowl. Find a pond or a creek with a good standing pool and fill your jar about one-quarter full with some debris from the bottom, followed by some low murky water. Most of the water life you will find lives down near the bottom. Now take a small handful of hay and lay it on the top of the water in your jar; drop in a few grains of charcoal for a deodorizer; and place a screen or thin piece of netting across the top.

After your infusion sits overnight, the murky water will have had a chance to settle, and you will be able to see the larger creatures climbing up on stems or coming to the top. Keep your eyes open for the nymphs of mayflies, dragonflies, damselflies, small water bugs, or possibly a caddisfly house that you may have gathered from the bottom debris.

All the life within your infusion will be feeding on and thriving from the nutrients released from the hay that you have added to the water. Within a few days you will have a population of microscopic and semimicroscopic creatures thriving within your jar of water.

After three or four days have passed, take an eyedropper and put a couple of drops of the water (preferably from the bottom of the jar) on a glass microscope slide with a cover slip on top. By scanning the slide under the scope, you will discover a whole new unseen world just teeming with life. It will be helpful to get a simple field guide to pond life or freshwater biology so you can become

a) Green Alga (*Spirogyra* sp.)

Protozoans:

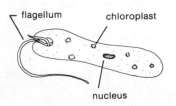

b) *Euglena spirogyra*

flagellum   chloroplast

nucleus

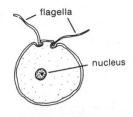

flagella

nucleus

c) *Chlamydomonas* sp.

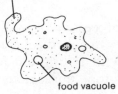

pseudopod

food vacuole

d) *Amoeba proteus*

e) *Spirostomum* sp.

f) *Vorticella* sp.

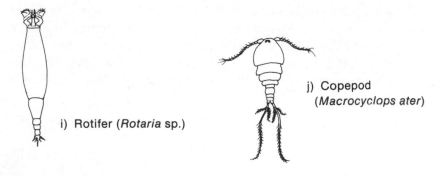

g) Cladoceran (*Daphnia pulex*)
(after Pennak)

h) Ostracod or bivalve seed
shrimp (*Cypridina* sp.)
(after Barnes).

i) Rotifer (*Rotaria* sp.)

j) Copepod
(*Macrocyclops ater*)

acquainted with and more easily able to recognize what you are seeing.

It may seem difficult to gain access to a microscope, yet you will find that most universities or high schools will let you use their equipment on the school premises. You might be able to make arrangements to work in an unused classroom or lab at certain times during the week; that way you will be able to learn the most from your hay infusion.

Following is a simple guide to some of the creatures you might find.

RAISING TADPOLES

Metamorphosis is quite a fascinating process, one that is well worth the time and effort necessary to observe it. Just imagine a small swimming creature with a long tail for locomotion that in a very short span of time miraculously becomes a four-legged, tailless frog!

You can temporarily observe this process by creating your own tadpole aquarium. Usually in April tadpoles can first be seen swimming along pond edges in the quieter water. When looking for areas where toads and frogs breed, keep your eyes open for their clear, jellylike eggs. The eggs of toads will be laid in strings, while frogs lay their eggs in masses. They can be collected with a small mesh net or, if you are especially quick, by dipping a large jar beneath them.

Before you find your tadpoles you will need to take a two-quart glass jar or fishbowl and arrange a layer of mud, leaves, stones, plants, and bottom debris from the edge of the pond in it. Fill the jar with pond water and let it sit until all the debris has settled to the bottom. Add about six tadpoles to their new home.

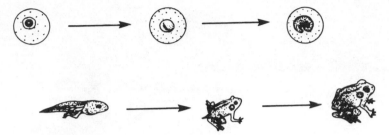

In order to feed the newly developing fellows, add some algae, some plant material from the pond, or a slimy stone each week. Watch the tadpoles dip toward these sources for nourishment.

As your tadpoles continue to grow and change into full-grown frogs, keep a record of illustrations showing their progressive changes. This is sure to be a rewarding project—enhance it by releasing your soon-to-be-mature frogs back into their native pond when your observations are complete.

UNDERWATER WONDERS

When walking by a creek or pond, we can easily see what is happening on the surface. The rippling waters of the creek, water striders skimming along the top, and the occasional splash of a fish coming to the surface are all exciting things to see.

Yet what is going on way below the areas we see casually in passing? One way to find out and to help us zoom in on some special areas is to build ourselves an underwater telescope. You'll feel just like the captain of a submarine as you peer through your scope in search of hidden creatures in the waters below.

To make your underwater scope you will need something tube-shaped and waterproof. A smooth-edged can works well, but be careful not to get one with sharp edges!

The longer the can the better, for that means you can explore even deeper in the water.

Take your can and remove the top and bottom so you have a tube that is open at both ends. Over one end place a piece of clear cellophane as tightly as you can; secure it in place with a rubber band. This will create a screen effect as you place it underwater, making the images of all you see much sharper and clearer.

Once your scope is completed, take it with you to the edge of a pond, creek, or stream; kneel down or lie on your stomach on the bank, being especially careful not to fall in. (When observing near water it is always a good idea to have a companion with you to share in the excitement and also to hold your feet!)

Incredible new worlds will open up to your eyes as you see all the hidden lives beneath the water scurrying to and fro. If you are out on an ankle-deep water ramble, be sure to take your scope with you so you can explore the life in the center of the creek, too.

Chapter 8
Moon Walks: Watching Nature After Dark

As the sun slowly sets and night begins to fall, a whole new world of life appears. The world of the night often seems mysterious, for many of us use our homes and shelters to protect us from what we cannot see. Yet what our eyes can't see, our other senses can detect if we just know what to look for. The world of the night creatures, both large and small, is fascinating and well worth exploring.

USHERING IN THE NIGHT

The following is a guide to just what you might hear, smell, or possibly faintly see in our forests and fields as night falls. As we explore life after dark we will also be exploring our senses; we must learn to use them to observe the unseen more effectively. The night need not be quite so mysterious if we just know a few of the more common sights and sounds we may encounter.

a) Raccoon

b) Flying squirrel

c) Glow worm (after Arnett)

d) Wolf spider.

A FEW TECHNIQUES

An overwhelming number of creatures come out after dark: Down in the grass many small insects are scurrying; through the woods large and small mammals such as mice, raccoons, and bears are hunting; and high above, the owls are watching for their dinner to scoot by.

Here are a few ideas you might try to make it easier for you to spot some of the creatures at work and play.

The life of the night is a seldom seen, mysterious world of sounds and smells. Once in a while one of these night critters will make a daytime appearance as did this barn owl on an early spring day.

The first thing you might try is to "think" like a woodland animal. Imagine you are a tiny mouse in the leaves at the base of a tree, and you know that somewhere up above a wise old owl is looking for a mouse just like you for supper. What will you most likely do? Of course—you'll be very quiet. If you can master the art of being oh, so quiet in the woods, you'll find it much easier to get closer to wild-life.

If you need a little extra light to see what's going on around you, try using a red-covered flashlight. The red beam is not seen by most night creatures, as their eyes do not have the color-sensitive cells that day creatures have, and the red appears black to them. A piece of red plastic or cellophane tied over the end of a flashlight will work well. Remember, though, this technique works best when you find yourself a quiet place to sit and observe and become one with nature.

You will now find a list of different signs you might come across in the night that may be telltale hints indicating the presence of some small or large creature out on an evening prowl.

The signs will be listed in the left column, with the names of the critters that would make these signs in the right column. The only trick is that the animals and plants in the right column are all mixed up; your challenge will be to match up the two columns so the sign is matched to the critter that would make it. If you get stuck, the answers are at the end of the series.

When you are finished, you will have a handy reference guide to some of the many life forms of the night world. This guide will include the most common things you might run across on your night exploration; there are actually hundreds of different creatures of all sizes and shapes that travel by night in our forests and fields.

Nature's Telltale Signs

1. Tree branches waving   a. Whippoorwills
2. Flash of white tails   b. Mice, shrews
   moving high off the
   ground
3. Flash of white tails   c. Rabbit
   moving low to the
   ground

4. Darting, zigzag movements in the air   d. Owls.

5. Darting movements through grass   e. Deer

6. Ghostlike wings bearing heavily feathered bodies   f. Skunks

7. Circling, fluttering movements of small bodies on the ground   g. Bats, moths

8. Black and white streaks moving about 6–12 inches above the ground   h. Possible storm

Night Lights

1. Gleaming points of lights in pairs   a. Raccoon

2. Flashes of light in the air   b. Beetle grubs

3. Tiny rows of light on the ground   c. Eyes

4. Bits of light glowing in rotten logs   d. Bullfrog

5. Green eyes glowing like opals   e. Glowworms

6. Bright yellow eyes   f. Noctuid moths

7. Small orange-red eyes shining on tree trunks   g. Fireflies

Nighttime Sounds

1.	Cooing whistle followed by a purr	a.	Bullfrog
2.	Deep boom like a heartbeat	b.	Spring peeper
3.	Loud hiss	c.	Wild boar
4.	Soft bleating	d.	Male striped skunk
5.	Deep, loud moan, growl, or grunt	e.	Ruffled grouse
6.	Honking from sky or pond	f.	Alarmed whitetail deer
7.	Croaking at night from trees	g.	Opossum, barn or barred owl
8.	Bass, bellowing sound from pool	h.	Female deer calling young
9.	Guttural grunts	i.	Canada geese
10.	Shrill screams	j.	Crows, ravens
11.	Whistling snort	k.	Wounded rabbit
12.	Yaps and yelps together	l.	Turtle falling in pool
13.	Solid plunk like large rock hitting water and sinking	m.	Foxes
14.	High, whistling "preep, preep, preep" in cadence	n.	Black bear

Nighttime Odors

1.	Strong and faintly sweet	a.	Fir
2.	Aromatic and spicy	b.	Fox, dog

3. Tangy and piny   c. Honeysuckle
4. Musty   d. Shrew
5. Rich and earthy   e. Spicebush
6. Faintly musky and doggy   f. Skunks
7. Very strong to nauseating   g. Ground after warm rain
8. Strongly musky, coming from dead leaves   h. Decaying leaves, mushrooms

Key

Nature's Telltale Signs

1.h   2.e.   3.c   4.g   5.b   6.d   7.a   8.f

Night Lights

1.c   2.g   3.e.   4.b   5.d   6.a   7.f

Nighttime Sounds

1.d   2.e   3.g   4.h   5.n   6.i   7.j   8.a   9.c   10.k
11.f   12.m   13.l   14.b

Nighttime Odors

1.c   2.e   3.a   4.h   5.g   6.b   7.f.   8.d

The next time you're sitting outside after dark, take a moment to close your eyes, take a deep breath, and listen to the wonders of life around you. Isn't it reassuring to know it's all out there!

ASTRONOMY CRAFTS

Here is an imaginative exercise that works well with five people or more. Probably one of the most-asked questions in the world of astronomy would be, "Is there life on other planets?" This art session won't answer that question, but it will provide a chance for you to let your imagination go and consider various possibilities for life in our universe.

Give everyone in the group a piece of paper and a pencil. Each person is to write down a description of a make-believe planet, telling its temperature, climate, what grows there, and any weird details they can think of to help paint a picture of this place. For instance, the planet I'm describing never goes over 10°F during the day; there are many trees, but they never grow any higher than eight inches. Every day at noon a tornado passes through, followed by a ten-minute snowstorm. This is just a short description; you could become much more elaborate if you wish.

After each person is finished creating a description, collect them all, fold them up, and then have everyone draw one out of a box, being sure no one gets his or her own.

Now comes the fun part: Using any medium you wish (pencil, crayon, paint, etc.), each person now tries to dream up a creature that would live on a planet like the one described on the sheet they drew. The results can be fun and amazing!

LEARNING CONSTELLATIONS—STARGAZING BY DAY AND NIGHT

Stargazing in the daytime? Is that possible? In a round-about way, this is the time for preparation. To get ready for the grand star show of the night sky, you could do a little research activity during the light hours.

The constellations are fascinating to study, associated as they are with so much folklore and so many fascinating stories of the gods, goddesses, and creatures that are said to live in the world of the stars. The American Indians have developed some beautiful legends about the "people" who live in the sky. By learning these legends along with the star patterns associated with these constellations, it becomes much easier to learn your way around the night sky. With a little practice and study, you can learn the sky as easily as you know your way around your town.

The American Indian related a beautiful legend about a group of stars called the Pleiades, or seven brothers. This constellation is very distinct, for it looks just like a little kite in the sky. The legend tells of seven boys who liked to play a game with stones, playing so often that they neglected their work in the cornfield. Their mothers would scold them repeatedly, but it did no good. So one day the mothers boiled the stones with their corn for dinner. When the boys came home they were hungry, yet when they sat down to eat their mothers dished them out the stones, saying, "Since you like these better than the cornfield, they will be your dinner." The boys were furious and stormed out, saying they would to go a place where they would be troubled no more. They began to do a dance called the feather dance, circling round and round, praying to the spirits for help. The mothers became afraid that something was wrong and rushed out after them, but alas, they were

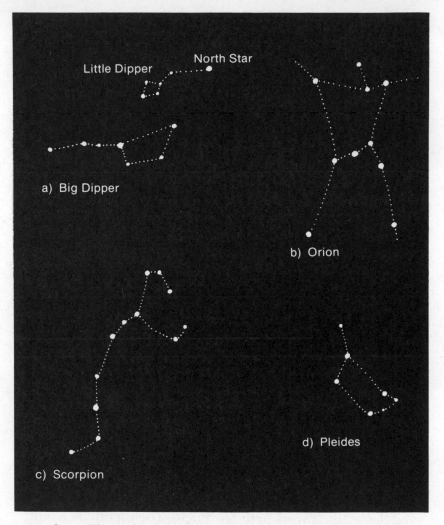

a) Big Dipper

North Star

Little Dipper

b) Orion

c) Scorpion

d) Pleides

too late. They reached the dancing boys just as their feet left the earth; they floated higher and higher with each round of dancing. The mothers ran to get them, but they were now too high to reach. Only one mother was able to grab one boy with a pole, but he struck the ground with such force that he sank into it and the earth closed over him. The other six continued to rise into the sky, where we see them now as the Pleiades. The people grieved over their lost sons, and the mother whose boy had sunk into the ground came and cried at that spot every day until the ground was damp with tears. Suddenly, a little green shoot sprouted and grew into the tree we now call the pine, which is of the same nature as the stars and holds in itself the same bright light.

This is but one of the many legends told about the stars and constellations of our universe. Have each person in your group learn a legend about a particular constellation as a daytime research project. One evening, as the sun begins to set, find yourself a nice quiet spot under the clear night sky, and let each person try to pinpoint his or her constellation and relate its special story.

A FULL-MOON WALK

Because the night is so mysterious and somewhat secretive, and since we are basically day creatures, the full moon enables us to become a part of the night world, since we are able to see a little better.

Deep within the woods the forest takes on a very different quality as the moonlight filters through the leaves and branches of the trees. An ideal place to enjoy the wonders of a moonlit night is in an open meadow, grassland, or field, where visibility is best.

In a full-moon walk there is the potential for an inspirational experience for yourself and all involved. This is a time of reflection, thought, and inner experience, for the night can be ever so quiet. Sometimes the only sounds around you may be the whispering of the wind through the trees or the peeping of a nearby insect in the grass.

This is a good time to discuss the life of the night—who is out there; what are they doing? The owl is hunting for his evening meal, the songbirds of the day are now setting their nests, and the fox is probably out stalking a late-night snack. Let your imagination go and while staring out into the nighttime air, talk about the animals, insects, and even plants. What are they doing after the sun falls and we are normally asleep?

Most importantly, though, after some quiet discussion, this is the ideal time for quiet personal reflection. I recall a very special group that joined me several years ago on a full-moon walk across the open balds of Roan Mountain. This night had promised a beautiful, clear, full moon, yet just an hour before sunset, what rolled in but a thunderstorm! As the storm passed, the fog started to rise; pretty soon the top of the mountain and the full moon were completely out of sight. It was certainly hard to decide what to do with fifty people who wanted to go to the highest peaks (possibly in the fog!) and enjoy the wonders of the full moon.

The whole group got together and took a vote, and everyone decided to take the chance and drive to the top. So off we went, through thick fog and misty air. The closer we got to the top, the more we began to worry that we'd never see the moon that night. Then all of a sudden we drove right out of the top of the clouds, and the sky above us was as clear as crystal.

The views we were blessed with at this point were nearly indescribable. At our feet were layers of clouds so thick they looked like you could walk on them. At the farthest edge of the clouds the sun was just finishing its final descent, with shades of red, yellow, and orange reflecting on the top cloud layers, putting on a color show as spectacular as a summer rainbow. Needless to say, everyone was speechless as they viewed this spectacle, quite a special surprise after driving through such thick fog!

Yet this was only the beginning. After this extra-special treat, we proceeded to the top of the mountain with clear sky above, to be greeted by the rising of the fullest orange moon I had ever seen.

We gathered in a group and started to walk across the top of the balds, mountains so open and treeless you could see for miles and miles in every direction. The moonlight was so bright that the highest ridges of the surrounding mountains were as clear to the eye as on a bright sunlit day.

When we reached the top of the ridge the speechlessness of the group told the story—the moods of the night had truly captured the hearts and minds of us all. Venturing into the night had proven to be a new and special type of nature study.

There may not be open bald mountains to cross during the coming of the full moon near where you live, but remember, that is not the main ingredient; the night and the moon are the important factors. This can be your special time as an individual or with a group, becoming a part of our natural world in a usually unexplored time frame.

STAR RELAY

Another way to learn the constellations is by playing a star relay game. Before starting to play it is a good idea to spend some time studying the constellations. Learn some of the basic ones as a group, for in this game team effort is what counts.

Two teams are chosen, and each player is given a paper star. If there are lot of players, one star each will be enough; but if there are only six or fewer members on each team, then you will need two stars each. Chose a leader; he or she should know the star patterns of each of the constellations that will be used in the game.

To begin the play, the leader calls out the name of a constellation. The members of each team get together and quickly try to lay their stars in a pattern that resembles that constellation. The first team to correctly create their paper constellation scores a point, and the play begins again with the leader calling out another constellation.

At the end of the game, the team that has scored the most points is declared the "top star," receiving a giant paper star with the team members' names printed on it.

Chapter 9
Snow Walks: Enjoying Winter's Delights

Here comes the snow . . . and what a cold chill it can bring. Curling up indoors by a warm fire makes it seem as though all life outside has come nearly to a halt until the return of the spring months. Yet there is still a world of activity and discovery to be found, even on the coldest days. Try a few of the activities described below and see what wonders a lovely snowy day can hold!

ANIMAL TRACKING

Taking a walk after a new snow falls can be peaceful and filled with a very special, quiet beauty. The silence of a falling snow can give you the feeling that you are the only one alive and journeying down whatever path you have chosen. Yet if you look a little closer, you might find that other creatures are out too, possibly hunting for a bite to eat or searching for a new place to keep warm.

Keep your eyes peeled to the ground for signs of animal tracks, for they can tell quite a story of life that

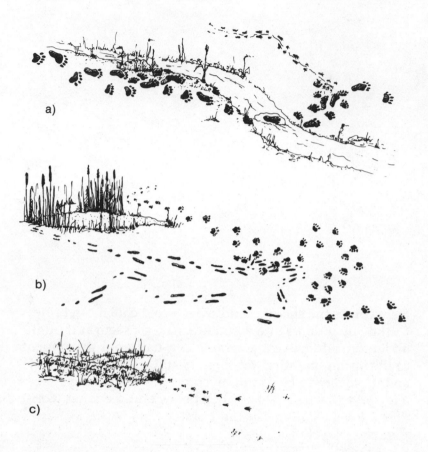

a)

b)

c)

goes on sometimes out of our sight. The passing of a fox could have taken place just moments before your arrival, the wildlife scattering at the first sign of your oncoming presence.

Mice, rats, squirrels, and rabbits are what are called bounding animals, traveling at a gallop of sorts. With each bound, prints are made by all four feet. In every case, the prints of the two hind feet are side by side, *in front* of the prints made by the forefeet.

There are also those animals that run on their toes. These are the animals such as the bobcat, house cat, dog, and fox, who tend to run as much as they walk. A cat's print fall in a single line, one before the other. Claw marks are absent in the track of a cat, for it walks with its claws retracted. On the other hand, the fox does not retract its claws, so claw marks are present; the prints occur in a single line like the cat's, but with much smaller toe pads.

A few animals walk with a much slower and more deliberate gait, touching both their toes and heels to the ground. Finding what looks like a baby's footprint in the muddy bank by a stream is probably a sign of a skunk. A track of a forefoot resembling a tiny hand with long spreading toes is the mark of a raccoon. The tiny shrew is interesting in that it appears to plant its whole body in the snow as it goes about eating its own weight in insects every day. It seems to travel in a groove, disappearing occasionally into snow tunnels and reappearing to form another groove.

The white-footed mouse, like the opossum, leaves its mark by dragging its tail. In deep snow, a brush mark at one side of a trail of tracks is the sign of a fox.

Following is a guide to some of the more common animal tracks you may encounter. These are presented in a slightly different fashion. Each animal you are tracking is out on a winter adventure, possibly meeting up with a predator that would like to have it for dinner, or you might be tracking a bird picking up seed which suddenly flies away. Watch their paths closely and see if you can discover what story has unfolded on this woodland trek.

WINTER TRAILS

Whenever the opportunity comes up, it is wonderful to be able to take advantage of a clear, brisk winter day. Wrap up warmly and head to the woods with some friends for this winter trail hunt.

As in a game of hide and seek, you will be exercising

your ability to observe signs in the woods and follow a trail made by one of your friends.

One person is chosen as the "trail maker," preferably one who knows the area you are exploring rather well. This person gets about a fifteen-minute head start and takes off into the woods along a familiar trail. As the trail maker goes, he or she is to leave very discreet signs of his passing without damaging anything in his path. For instance, he may leave a very definite footprint in some soft soil, push a few downed leaves into a tiny pile, break a dead limb hanging over the trail from a nearby tree, or maybe turn over a small rock.

The "trail hunters" will proceed down the trail behind the trail maker, carrying with them pieces of brightly colored string or yarn to tie on branches to mark the places where they have spotted the trail maker's signs. When they get to the end of the allotted trail they will find the trail maker waiting for them, and as they return back up the trail together they can remove the strings as they go, the trail maker checking to see if they spotted all his well-placed signs.

Animals make many signs very similar to what you may be following. By learning to recognize discreet disturbances on the ground or nearby you will be able to spot the passing of a deer, raccoon, or any other creature that may have traveled the same route you have chosen.

OBSERVATION DRAWING

You awake one morning to a new-fallen snow, knowing you have to head out to work or school and venture through the drifts. Do you ever wonder just how much you noticed, or were you in too much of a hurry to really appreciate the natural wonders that unfolded around you the night before?

For a little drawing exercise, ask yourself, your class, or your children the following questions. The answer to each question will be a sketch or drawing of just what your memory holds of the day's earlier observation.

1. How did the sky look before the snowfall?
2. How did the sky look during the snowfall?
3. How did the sky look after the snowfall?
4. What did the ground look like around your home before the snowfall?
5. What did the ground look like around your home after the snowfall?
6. While you were outside, where were the drifts the highest?
7. How many animals tracks did you notice?

SNOWFLAKE CATCHING

Snowflakes appear by the millions as they float through the air, then they seem to vanish into one solid mass as they accumulate on the ground. The beauty and intricacy of each individual snowflake are amazing; no two are alike, each and every one unique.

It's difficult to catch a snowflake in your hand to observe, for the heat of your body melts it away before you have a chance to really see it. Luckily, there are ways to slow the little fellows down so you can take the time to enjoy their delicate, soft outlines.

Keep a few sheets of black paper handy in your freezer so they are cold (construction paper will work well). As the snow begins to fall, hold your black paper out under

a) Plate

b) Star (stellar)

c) Needle

d) Column/plate (combination often called a "cuff-button").

the sky to let a few flakes land on it. They will not last a long time, but they should survive long enough for you to get a much closer look at their crystallizing patterns and perhaps even sketch a few on a white sheet of paper before they melt away. If a microscope is available, put your black paper and snowflake under the scope for a very special closeup look at the tiny details.

To demonstrate how different each snowflake is, give everyone a sheet of paper folded in half several times (but not too thick to cut). Take your scissors and clip little corners, circles, lines, and odd shapes along the folded edges of the paper. When each person is finished, he or she can unfold the snowflakes; you will see that each is completely individual!

WHERE DID THEY GO? HOMES IN WINTER

As the ground starts to freeze and we proceed into the winter months, we may wonder what has happened to our forest friends.

One of the smaller creatures, the spider, has many interesting ways of surviving cold weather. Some of the young spiders are born in great numbers inside egg cases in the fall. Rather than journey out into the world, they stay within the security of their tiny egg house. A winter food source is provided as the spiderlings prey upon each other. When the warmth of spring arrives, the strong surviving spiders emerge into the world. Adult spiders can be found hiding in cracks of buildings, bedding down under the leaf litter of the forest, or possibly living down in the roots of the mosses. Certain species, such as the daddy longlegs, survive the winter by depositing eggs, since most of the adults die.

As late summer and fall approach, many animals prepare to hibernate for the winter. The raccoon, groundhog, eastern chipmunk, jumping mouse, and bat are the most common hibernators of the Southern Appalachians. They spend their last warm months storing excess amounts of fat in their bodies to help nourish and sustain them until spring. Those animals observed in hibernation have been found to need little oxygen or food, as they breathe very slowly and unevenly, while their body temperature approaches that of their surrounding environment. The black bear and the red squirrel are sometimes called *semiactive*. They do hibernate, but when a winter warm spell rolls around they will be up and wandering.

Salamanders, newts, and toads are another group of hibernators. Many leave the creeks and streams and head to the fields, while others remain in the creeks in the bottom silts and sands. The toads burrow their way anywhere between three to four inches and three to four feet into the soft soil of pond banks. Always thinking to the future, they burrow in backward so they can come out head first in the spring!

Frogs seem to find a variety of homes for the winter:

Some head for tree cavities, some retreat beneath leaves and stones on the forest floor, and some, like the American bullfrog, burrow into the stream bottoms.

Snakes are an interesting group, as they not only hibernate but are said to migrate, too. There are many who claim that some varieties of snakes have common denning grounds and will migrate to the same spot yearly. They may stay close to the surface or up to three feet below the ground in clusters of rocks. They conserve moisture and warmth by forming hibernating balls composed of many entwined bodies of snakes.

The great majority of mammals in the Southern Appalachians do tend to remain active rather than falling into a hibernating state. The red fox, bobcat, gray squirrel, rabbit, and deer continue to seek food and shelter throughout the winter months. Evidence of their presence can be found after a new-fallen snow, when their tracks may be spotted scurrying to and fro across a carpet of white.

Do a little research into the animals of your area, discovering where they go as the weather turns cold.

You can play a fun game of tag with the players representing different animals. Each animal is safe only when he or she is at the correct winter den. Hang labels on objects in the playing area that represent these winter homes. For example, the player who is the frog will be safe only when he is touching the tree labeled "pond," the bear is safe only when he is touching the rock labeled "tree," and the northern birds are safe when they are touching the tree labeled "South." One person is "it"; he or she chases the other animals. As they are caught, they join "it" in trying to tag the other animals. The last remaining animal is declared the winner and gets to choose the next game.

Chapter 10
Bringing It All Together

As you have become involved in the activities of previous chapters you have found yourself awakening your senses, from discovering the smallest forms of life to investigating the mysteries of those tiny points of light in the sky above.

Keep your senses keen and your mind open as you begin the games, crafts, group participation ideas, workbooks, and the many activities that follow. It is here you can draw from the experiences you have had while engaging in the activities within this book and those that have left impressions in your life.

Remember, as you become involved in what is to follow, all the creatures we have acquainted ourselves with as we discovered everything from the little guys in the pond to the birds of the air. Above all, keep your imagination wide open as you learn, share, and experience new things with others.

GAMES FOR THE NATURE LOVER

Leaf-Passing Relay

Every part of our natural world, no matter how strong, can be very fragile when inconsiderately abused by man.

This relay stresses just how fragile nature can be. If we as caretakers of this land do not think before we act, the results can sometimes be irreparable.

Form two or more teams, with at least four members per team. The object of the relay is to successfully pass a leaf from the front of the line to the rear in an over-and-under fashion, with each member facing forward. The first person passes the leaf between his legs, the second person passes it over his head, the third passes it between his legs, and so on. When the leaf reaches the last person in line, he is to run to the front of the line with the leaf; the passing process is repeated until each member has started at the front of the line.

You have to be very, very careful with your leaf—for if it is injured in any way, the entire team is disqualified and loses the relay. The first team to pass their leaf successfully through the series without harming it is the winner.

Opposites and Alternates

This is a two-team game that is fun and also requires a little thought. Before actually playing the game, an introduction to trees would be helpful. Take a short hike and spend some time observing the leaf and branch patterns of the different trees in your area. Notice how some trees have opposite leaves, while others are alternate.

Recognizing this difference is the first step in learning to distinguish the different types of trees. You may want to teach your group some names of trees while you are preparing for this game.

Opposite

a) Ash (*Fraxinus* sp.)

b) Maple (*Acer* sp.)

c) Flowering dogwood (*Cornus florida*)

d) Buckeye (*Aesculus* sp.)

Alternate

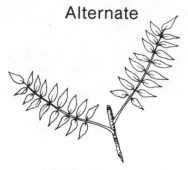

e) Walnut (*Juglans* sp.)

f) Oak (*Quercus* sp.)

g) Hickory (*Carya* sp.)

h) Beech (*Fagus* sp.)

To play, try to divide your group into two equal teams. Team 1 is the "opposite" team; team 2 is the "alternate" team. You, or someone elected as the leader (the leader cannot be on a team), calls out either "opposite" or "alternate." If the opposite team is called, they must run from the alternate team and are safe only when they tag a tree with opposite leaves. Every member of the opposite team who is tagged before reaching a safe place has to join the alternate team. When everyone reaches a safe spot, the first play is over and both teams reassemble.

The process is repeated again, with the leader calling "opposite" or "alternate." If they call "alternate," the play is the same except the alternate team is not safe until they tag a tree with alternate leaves. In this case everyone tagged by the opposites before reaching their safety zone must join the other team.

The game continues until either the opposites or alternates have captured all the other team members.

Crawdad Tag

Ever tried to walk like a crayfish? It's probably something we don't try every day, but it sure makes for a good game!

Sometimes we take for granted the challenges different creatures must meet simply to survive in their environment; the crawdad is no exception. Imagine living in an ever-flowing river or creek where you must constantly battle the force of the water to eat and exist.

In playing this game, the players get a chance to experience a more difficult kind of movement; they will begin to appreciate some of the unusual ways in which other creatures must move to get around.

Before beginning the play, sometimes a little practice is helpful. All players will be walking on all fours, with their backs to the ground and their bellies to the sky. Every-

Getting about is not quite as easy when you become a creek critter playing Crawdad Tag!

one will be moving with a slight upside-down waddle in this awkward position. After a short practice in this position, it is time for the game.

All players are divided into two teams, the "crawdads" and the "snakes." (Queen snakes like to dine on young crayfish.) The object of the game is for the snakes to tag the crawdads while both teams are moving in this upside-down fashion. There is no home base; play continues until all crawdads are captured. Captured crawdads become snakes.

The last remaining crawdad is the "elder" of his team; he becomes the one to choose a new team for the next game.

Turtle Relay

It takes quite a cooperative effort to be a turtle. We'll find this out as three or four people try to become one under a shell.

You will need a piece of cardboard, a large box, or a large sheet of paper, big enough to cover the three or four people that you are trying to get under it. The box or paper will be the shell of the turtle.

You can make as many turtles as you wish, as long as there are three or four people under each shell. Each turtle will be trying to exist as one unit, for it would fall to pieces if one foot tried to go to the right while the other went off to the left.

There is one ingredient missing—that is the predator. You may have as many predators as turtles; the object is for each predator to tag a turtle's toes or fingers only. The turtle in turn is trying to keep his toes and fingers tucked under his "shell" so the predator can't catch him.

All the turtles start at one point, with a specific destination or finish line in mind. Give the turtles a short head start and then release the predators, reminding the turtles to keep their toes and fingers tucked in their shells. The predators are not allowed to pull the shells off the turtles in any way. They can only wait for the turtle to slip out from under the edge and then tag him.

If the turtle is tagged the predator is the winner, but if the turtle makes it to his destination the predator loses the relay.

Dinner Time—Food Chains and How They Work

It's hard to grasp the idea that in our natural world everybody eats somebody or something else at some time or another in order to survive. Before beginning the game, try discussing with your group just what it is that we eat and where it comes from. It may be a little easier to understand how our natural world exists by first discussing what *we* do to survive. For example, ask everyone, "What do you eat?" Your second question might be, "How did your dinner grow?" For instance, if you eat vegetables, they grew by the light and energy of the sun, water, and nu-

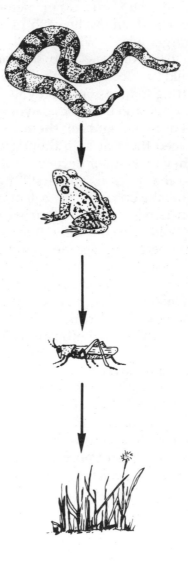

trients from the soil. You may go a bit further and ask how the water got into the soil and so on. Before you know it you have verbally created a food chain.

Now it is time to begin the game. There may be between five and twenty players, with each player portraying a plant, animal, or natural element. Encourage some to be animals, some plants, and a few to play the parts of the soil, rain, clouds, sun, and other elements necessary to create a complete chain. Make each player a name tag so no one will forget who is what.

The fun part comes as you tie yourselves together trying to "build" a food chain. You will need a large ball of twine or string to help construct your chain. Have your group form a circle and then pick anyone at random, hand them the ball of twine, and ask them which person in the group could feed them or help them grow.

When they make their decision, ask them to toss the ball gently to that person, while still holding the end of the twine. Now the one with the ball of twine must decide which person is necessary for *their* survival. When they decide, they hold onto the unwound twine and toss the ball to the next person; the game continues until everyone has caught the ball at least once.

In the center of the circle there will be a very intricate food "web" illustrating just how complex the interactions within our natural world really are. After you have discussed this and admired the beautiful web all have constructed, ask the question, "What would happen if a part of our web were removed?"

To illustrate this, clip the string at one person, trying to pick a spot important to most of the others. If someone is playing the part of the air, clip it there and ask how people harm their air and if we would be able to live without it. Of course, when you clip the string and remove one part, the web will collapse, showing nature's fragility.

Rainbow Scavenger Hunt

A scavenger hunt for a rainbow? This is a very special hunt in which you will use your eyes and imagination as a means to find all the colors of the rainbow somewhere out in Mother Nature's domain.

Any number can play; all that is necessary is a piece of paper and a pencil for each player. The object of the game is to find as many natural things as you can that match the different colors of the rainbow and to list them on your sheet of paper.

Across the top of each sheet, write each color of the rainbow: red, orange, yellow, green, blue, indigo, and violet, marking columns beneath each color.

Within a designated area, each "hunter" ventures out, trying to spot as many of these different rainbow colors as they can, listing them in the appropriate columns.

At the end of the hunt have each person share what they have found with the others. It will be amazing how one person will see something that the others may not. You might like to have a special certificate or award for the winner and best observer.

The Spider and the Fly

Before the start of this game, a string web must be constructed. It doesn't need to be a circular web, but a path of string that goes from tree to post to stake to tree, and so on. Make sure this is in an area where there is nothing to trip over, for the players will be blindfolded. At some points, make intersections in the string where it overlaps each others' paths. (see illustration). The spider's path should be strung about waist high so it can be followed by running your hand along it and still standing upright.

The object of the game is for the spider to find the fly. First, a blindfold is placed on the spider, then the fly

finds himself a place somewhere in the web; he cannot move from there throughout the play. The fly must be very quiet, for he does not want the spider to find him. The spider only has one or two minutes (depending on the size of the web) to find the fly. He will find it very helpful to stop and listen carefully for any sound the fly might make rather than traveling haphazardly through the web. Any spectators should be asked to be quite silent so their sounds will not distract the spider.

At the end of the allotted time, if the fly has not been found he may go free; the spider then becomes the next fly, with a new spider being chosen. If the spider has found the fly, the fly has become the spider's dinner, and both a new spider and fly are chosen for the next play.

The Fox and the Bird

In order to play this game at least ten players are necessary. Of them, one is chosen as the fox and another as the bird. All the remaining players are trees—they should form a circle, starting with their hands behind their backs. The fox is inside the circle, so he cannot see the hands of the trees. The bird is outside the circle.

The game begins as the bird, who is carrying a small rock that symbolizes an egg, walks around the circle saying,

"I have an egg within my nest,
Where can I hide it from the sly fox's quest?"

All the while the bird pretends to drop the egg in the hands of one of the trees. The bird should try to bluff the fox so he cannot tell which tree really has the egg. After the bird has left the egg somewhere she should stop; the fox must then guess which tree is holding the egg.

The fox only gets one guess; if he is correct he becomes the bird, the bird becomes a tree, and the tree holding the egg becomes a fox. If the fox is incorrect, he becomes a tree, the tree with the egg becomes the next fox, and the bird gets to hide her egg again.

After the bird has stumped three foxes, she becomes a tree and chooses a new bird to replace her.

Camouflage Hide and Seek

It is quite an art to be able to sit so silently and still that a small chipmunk will continue its foraging for food close to your spot. Learning to do this is one of the objects of the "hiders," who will try to remain unfound by the "seeker." One person in the group is a seeker; all the others are hiders. The seeker's job could be hard, depending on how well the others camouflage themselves.

The hiders need to become part of the forest. They might pretend to be a moth on the side of a tree, a small mouse behind a rock, or a tiny snake curled up under a bush, remembering all the while to stay absolutely still and try to become a part of the environment.

This will make a more challenging job for the seeker, as he must be especially alert and observant, listening for the slightest rustle or breath. As each hider is found, he or she will help find the others until they are all found.

NATURAL ARTS AND CRAFTS

Forest Finger Puppets

MATERIALS NEEDED: Scraps of material cut in approximately 3-by-4½-inch pieces

Construction paper of various colors

Felt-tip markers

Glue

Scissors

Yarn scraps

You can represent virtually anything your heart desires when making a finger puppet, from a tree to a bear, or even the sun!

Each person needs a piece of material, which should first be sized to the finger he or she will be wearing it on. To size it, lay your finger on the open square of cloth and fold it in half. If it is too loose, cut it a little smaller, then run a thin line of glue down the side to hold it together. By laying your finger on top of the material you can see how tall you want your puppet; then fold the excess over and glue it down (see illustration). Let your glue set and dry for about ten minutes before you proceed or your material will pull apart as you start to work on it.

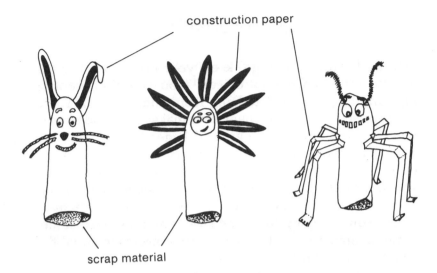

construction paper

scrap material

When your puppet form is dry you can begin decorating it, creating the image you desire on the front. Using construction paper, yarn scraps, and felt-tip markers, begin gluing the paper and yarn on to make your puppet. The markers will come in handy to draw on a face or whiskers. By using these three materials you can make yourself quite a fancy character to wear on your finger.

For an added game, try making up a puppet play to be acted out by everyone and their new finger puppets.

Fancy Mobiles

MATERIALS NEEDED: Pipe cleaners or sticks
String or thread
Scissors
Glue
Natural objects lying on the forest floor

Before beginning this project, a little scavenger hunt of sorts should be organized to obtain materials for your mobile. Take a little trek out into the woods, fields, or your

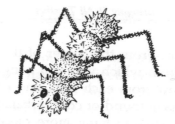

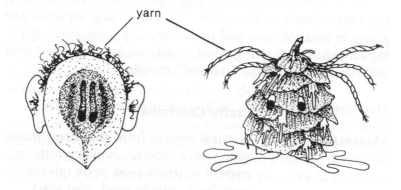

yarn

remembrance of him. Look around and see what you can find lying on the ground. All types of dried objects will work well to make your crafty creation.

The first step is to decide just what it is you want to make. Pick one of the creatures that you enjoy seeing when you're out. Larger objects such as pine cones, the various nuts, and some of the larger seeds or sticks can work well for the body. By using drops of glue the smaller things you've collected—such as pine needles, the propeller maple seeds, elm seeds, and so on—can be used. Your imagination is your only limit! Try using these materials for ears, eyes, tails, legs, and other appendages. You will need to hold some of the pieces in place until the glue dries so they don't drop off, but when you're finished you'll have yourself a brand new woodsy creation of your favorite creature!

A Nature Collage

MATERIALS NEEDED: A variety of natural objects found on the forest floor that will lie well on a piece of paper (fallen leaves, a little crumbled soil, small sticks, bark, fallen seeds from herbs or trees

A sheet of paper for each person

Glue

Anyone with an imagination can make a nature collage. You'll be surprised at what wonderful creations you can come up with using materials similar to those described above.

This project can be even more exciting if it is begun with a little nature ramble through the woods and fields, with each person on the ramble keeping his or her eyes peeled to the ground for unusual fallen objects. Try looking for appealing shapes and colors as you scan the earth around you, for that is what is going to make your collage especially exciting and different from all the rest. Pick up things that appeal to you as you see them, so when the ramble is over you will be prepared to begin your own personal collage.

When you have returned, find a flat surface to work on, such as a table or a level section of ground. Lay down your piece of paper and begin by spreading out the natural objects you have collected. Study them for a moment— notice the more unusual shapes, the different hues and tones, and the textures of your collection. Try arranging part or all of what you have collected on your piece of paper in a pleasing arrangement. You may want to develop a story relating your ramble through the woods, or you may prefer to approach your collage from an entirely visual perspective...how appealing is it as a shape and color creation?

The first pattern you arrange your collage in doesn't have to be the final project, either. Move things around until you are satisfied with the result. Then take your tube of glue and stick your objects to the paper so they will not fall off.

When you are finished you will have created a very beautiful and fragile piece of artwork, as fragile as nature itself. Handle it gently and you will have a very special remembrance of a special trip to the outdoors.

Rain Brush Paintings

MATERIALS NEEDED: Paper (any color)

Paint that is not quick drying—
tubes of acrylic or powdered
tempera paints work well

What to do on a rainy day when you really want to be outdoors? If you're feeling a creative streak on what would normally be an "indoor" day, try your hand at rain brush paintings. They are really very simple to make and a lot of fun, for you never really know just how your painting is going to turn out. How can that be? By using the very things that are keeping you inside you can come up with some beautiful and exciting, colorful paintings. Instead of using a paintbrush you'll be using the rain itself. Just imagine each tiny raindrop acting as a small precision brush, blending the colors of your painting.

Begin by deciding what colors you would like to use on your painting. If you use acrylic paint, squirt tiny blobs on your paper where you want them, spreading them only slightly (leave the paint a little thick). If you are using premixed tempera paints, apply colors very loosely, not thinning them out too much. The powdered tempera paints will create an interesting effect if you sprinkle the powder on your paper where you want it, then let the rain melt it down and mix the powdered colors for you!

As you work, remember: Once you start applying color to the paper you need to work quickly, for if the paint becomes dry, the rain's tiny brushes will not be able to blend your colors. If you are working with the powder, though, you will be able to spend more time, as the powder will not be dampened until the rain hits it.

It takes only a few seconds for the rain to do its job in finishing your design. How hard it is raining makes a big difference in how long it takes to wet your paper. Lay your painting in the rain for just a few seconds, then pull it back into a dry spot. Quickly decide if you like the way it looks or would like to let the rain paint it a little longer. You can do this several times if you'd like, just don't let your paper become so waterlogged that it falls to pieces.

When you have a finished product that you are happy with, put your picture somewhere to dry before you handle it too much. After your work is dry you will have a lovely rain-splatter painting created by your hands and Mother Nature's too!

Nature's Shadows

MATERIALS NEEDED: The bottom of a shoebox or old cigar box

Cardboard strips cut in widths to the depth of your box

Glue

Scissors

Colored construction paper

Some of your favorite nonliving
natural objects (pine cones,
attractive rocks, strangely shaped
sticks)

Tempera paint and brush

To begin, take your box and paint the outside edge and
back with tempera paint in the color of your choice. Paint
the inside of the box black. Measure your cardboard strips
to the same length as the surface that the box will be sitting
on—some like their shadowbox sitting in an upright position; others prefer it resting lengthwise along the table.
Whichever direction you choose, be sure to cut your strips,
which will be acting as little shelves, to the length of the
box plus one-half inch of overlap so you will have an area
to glue down.

You will be making an arrangement of shelves somewhat like a tic-tac-toe board, yet your finished product will
be much more attractive if you offset the shelves to avoid
such a square effect. Look at the objects you have collected
and wish to place on these shelves when it is finished so
you can plan for enough room in each little square to hold
the object.

After you have your long shelves glued in place, place
your natural objects on them and decide where to put your
upright cardboard strips to square in your shadowbox.
Refer to the illustration to see how your finished product
will look.

As you cut your upright strips, don't forget to leave
one-half inch extra length to use as a gluing surface to
attach the strip to the shelf and box edge.

Once the shadowbox is made you can arrange and
rearrange the objects inside, occasionally returning some
to the outdoors and gathering up new visitors to occupy
the shelves.

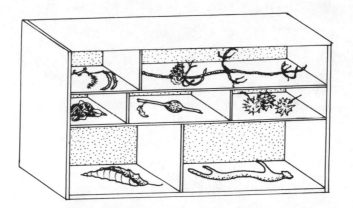

Try experimenting with lighting when you place your finished box in your room, as different angles will produce a different array of shadows from the objects inside.

GROUP PARTICIPATION IDEAS

There are many ways to draw large groups together into activities that will introduce them to and hopefully inspire them to take an interest in our environment and what they can do as individuals to help keep our natural world clean and as it should be. Some of the activities are competitive in a sense, while others require a more cooperative group effort.

Whichever one you try with your group, you may find that the team energies exerted in these activities may help the folks you work with to better understand and care for their environment.

Competitive Activities

NATURE AWARENESS CONTESTS

Putting your efforts into a contest can be exciting and rewarding for all participants. There are two types of contests that have worked well in activities I have conducted with

---

Who knows what questions might arise as your team travels from rock to tree on your adventures through the Trivial Maze?

large groups in Tennessee; I hope they will work well for you too.

1. Poster contests. There are so many themes that can be developed around poster designs—for instance, endangered habitats, endangered animals, my favorite place in nature, why preserve the environment, or themes involving current environmental problems.

Once you choose your theme, an allotted time should be set in which the group has to develop their ideas and complete their finished product. You may allow one week or two months, depending on how much research you would like to go into each poster. Any artist's medium could be acceptable, encouraging the use of pencil, paint, or even crayon, depending on the age group.

Be sure to display all posters that are turned in, for everyone will be very proud of their work and will surely want to show it off. Perhaps you'll want to present an award for the best poster.

Your group's work will open up a pathway for many discussions on different topics relating to each person's creation. Don't let this opportunity for discussion slip by, for this is an appropriate time for each person to learn the views of others on issues relating to our environment.

See if your group's work can be displayed publicly. There are many local organizations, clubs, libraries, and so on that would be more than happy to display an effort like this for others to view and enjoy.

2. Designing a button. A button design contest is similar to the poster contest in that each person participating will be developing a theme, as we mentioned previously. In designing a button, try to think of a particular statement you want to make; anyone who sees your button will also get your message so the design is very important. A button cannot be too "busy," or the reader will not be able to receive your message at a glance.

As with the poster contest, each person designs his or her button on a piece of paper, with the theme relating to nature or the environment. Once again, all the designs can be displayed publicly, but the real excitement of this contest is that the winner's design can be made into a button that everyone can wear!

If you have a nature club or group of any kind that is in need of a fund-raising activity, this will work very well. Each button can be sold for a small profit, which will benefit the work of your nature-conscious group. In addition, the project will instill a very special pride as each club member and the button's creator see something representing their work and involvement being worn on the clothes of folks all over your community.

WILDLIFE SPELLING BEE

Spelling bees are always exciting—who can resist a chance at the thrill of being one of the best spellers in the group, standing up there until the last word is asked!

The old-time spelling bee is a good way to bring the world of wildlife to your group in a very different light. Possibly a week before the assigned date of the bee you need to prepare and distribute a list of words that will be asked during the actual competition. Any word that has some relationship to wildlife, the environment, or any form of nature study is acceptable, with the degree of difficulty being geared toward the age of the group. By passing out the list at least a week before the bee, you give everyone the opportunity to study and ask questions about unfamiliar words.

The real joy of a spelling bee of this sort is the enormous opportunity it provides for discussion of all sorts of nature-related subjects. If you meet with your group on a regular basis—a school class, for instance—you might want

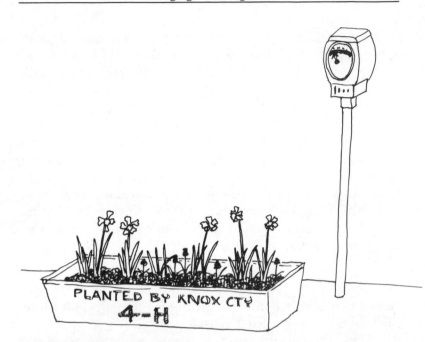

to discuss several of the words on the list each day prior to the spelling bee. Just imagine how you will open the door to discussion and discovery picking a word like "conservation" or "pollution" from the list and asking the group just what those words bring to mind.

For the actual spelling bee, the group should be divided into two nearly equal teams. The teams may want to choose a name for themselves, perhaps naming themselves for a favorite plant or animal. The first person is asked to spell a word from the list. He or she should first repeat the word, then spell it, then repeat the word again. If correct, the speller remains in his or her position in line; if the word is misspelled, the speller returns to his or her seat.

The next word is given to the first person on team 2, following the same procedure as previously described. This method continues, alternating from team 1 to team 2, until only one person is left on each team. There will be a winner on each team; they will compete against each other until one person has proven to be the top wildlife speller.

The grand prize winner and the opposing team winner each receive a prize for their excellent efforts. It is also nice to give a special participation award to everyone who entered the spelling bee, for they have probably shown a great deal of effort and interest over the previous week. Their insights into the realm of the natural world have probably changed dramatically thanks to your taking the time to open their eyes to many things either unseen or taken for granted.

OUTDOOR ALPHABETS

Played very similarly to the Wildlife Spelling Bee, Outdoor Alphabets is a bee with a twist.

Divide the group into two teams, with one person— possibly yourself—as leader. The game is played like a spelling bee, except each person is asked to name something nature-related beginning with each consecutive letter of the alphabet.

To begin, the first person on team 1 names something beginning with the letter *A* that has to do with nature, plants, or animals. (If you prefer, you can limit your subject matter to plants only, animals only, and so on.) Then the first person on team 2 must say team 1's word plus name something new beginning with the letter *B*. Next, the second person on team 1 must rename what was called for *A* and *B* and add something for the letter *C*. This continues until someone misses—for instance, if a player cannot recall all the previously named words. They are then out of the competition and must take a seat. The next person up on the opposite team must try to do what the previous person just missed. This continues until there is only one person left, and he or she is declared the winner. As an example, below is the beginning of the play, labeled as to each team and the player number.

Team 1, Player 1	"Apple"
Team 2, Player 1	"Apple, bear"
Team 1, Player 2	"Apple, bear, cactus"
Team 2, Player 2	"Apple, bear, cactus, den"

TRIVIAL MAZE

This is a game of questions and answers, with a team of people or one individual trying to find their way to the end of the trail. It's fun to play and a challenge to set up.

The organizer of the maze will be the person to lay it out, write the questions, and be sure that each question is appropriate (not too hard) for the group playing.

The leader will write a series of multiple-choice questions, possibly ten to twenty, each to be posted at station numbers corresponding to the question number. Your stations can be outdoors, posted on trees, rocks, fences, and so on, or around the inside of a home or school.

There will be two answers for each question; only one will be right. Each answer, whether it is right or wrong, will tell you where you should proceed from a certain point. For example, question 1 is tacked on a red oak tree, at station 1. The question asks, "Which of the following birds would you be most likely to see swooping from the sky to catch a mouse in the field?" Answers: A) Bluebird—proceed to station 6; B) Hawk—proceed to station 4. The team chooses and writes down the answer they think is correct and follows the instructions that accompany the answer. When they go to their next station they will be asked another multiple-choice question arranged in the same way as the example. The stations and answers must be arranged so that only the team that answers *all* the questions right will end up at station 10 (or the highest-numbered station), with a special surprise "You're a Winner!" to greet them instead of another question. If at any time someone answers a question wrong, that team will never make it to station 10. After making ten stops at ten stations, they will know they have missed at least one question in the group if they don't get to the winning station.

Cooperative Activities

No-Touch Scavenger Hunt

Scavenger hunts are great for allowing groups of all sizes to share the many new discoveries they make during a trip to the outdoors. In a no-touch scavenger hunt there is one very special rule—nothing is to be collected or brought back. Instead of carrying everything back with us, let's try a new method that is just as effective. The leader of the group needs to prepare a sheet that tells what each person will be hunting for—a discovery sheet (see illustration). They are not asked to find something as specific as a piece of moss, but instead might be asked to find something very soft and damp. This will give each person more of a chance to use the imagination; at the same time, you will find that different people have different concepts of what is soft and damp, and they can all be right!

Instead of bringing this soft, damp thing back from the hunt, each participant is given a pencil and is asked to sketch the thing they found on the paper in a space left next to the item on the list.

The hunt continues, with everyone wandering in a designated area, sketching the objects they have found that they feel represent what is asked for.

SCAVENGER HUNT

Discovery   sheet!

PLANTS
SKETCH
Leaf with veins shaped like a hand
Leaf with branched veins
A plant not more than 1" tall
A plant not more than ½" tall
A plant not less than 6 feet tall
A plant in bloom
A plant with seeds
A plant that doesn't die in winter
A mushroom
A plant growing on a tree
Find the best hugging tree
A "patch" of something (the same thing covering the area)

ANIMALS
SKETCH
A salamander
A critter that might live in a tree (big or little!)
A snail
A toad
A spider
Something that buzzes

MISCELLANEOUS
SKETCH
Something smooth and wet
Something rough
Something furry
A sweet odor
A sour odor
Something unnatural to the forest
Something you think would taste good (but don't try it!)
Something that would make a good seat

OTHER
Find your favorite spot . . .
   why did you choose this spot?

When all are finished, gather in a group and go through the list, letting each person share with the rest what it was they found while on their scavenger hunt. Everyone will be quite surprised as they discover that more than one thing fits each description, and that each thing discovered was just as good as the next!

HEADS-TOGETHER LITTER PICK-UP

It seems a shame that an activity like this one is even necessary, but as we view the roadsides of our country, the creek banks and the backwood trails, we seem to find in some of the most out-of-the-way places the remnants of those who felt that their litter should remain on the ground for others to view and, unfortunately, to clean up for them.

Through this activity an understanding of litter, what it is and what each and every one of us can do about it, is developed as a group pools their efforts to beautify an area that was once littered.

Several important concepts need to be brought out during an activity of this type. An understanding needs to be developed as to what litter is, where it comes from, and, worst of all, where it goes. Ask your group just how long they think a plastic milk jug will lie on the creek bank if someone doesn't pick it up. Most of the forms of trash we find scattered along our trails and roadways are not likely to decay anytime in the near future. Will an aluminum can rot back into the earth and provide the trees with the nutrition they need to survive? It is very doubtful. All it could give to the earth is its unsightly presence along with some chemical residue as it lies on the ground. It is also very unlikely that any living thing anywhere would even consider eating it . . . so its destiny is all too obvious.

These are but a few of the many subjects that could

As we have worked together we have made it possible for the tiny violet to bloom in a place free of litter.

be discussed as your group is engaged in cleaning the litter from an area. You may choose an area that all of you use on occasion, or you may prefer to volunteer your services to a local park or forest area that has been in need of cleanup. With everyone working together as a group to clean up an area, they will more greatly appreciate the value of keeping an area clean, for it is no easy job to pick up litter.

One of the biggest questions that will come up is, "How do we keep it clean now? Won't it just be littered again as time goes on?" The answer is maybe yes and maybe no, but the true value of the group's efforts is the important aspect of this activity. Each and every person involved has set a very special example for the rest of the community, that they *do* care and that they need everyone's help to make these efforts work.

Each person in your group can vow that in the future they will not litter, and if they see others littering, they can in a very polite way ask them not to dirty our environment.

To keep our world clean will take the cooperative effort of each person living on earth. By enlightening your group, you will have helped save a portion of the world from further pollution.

MAPPING

Arranging your thoughts and observations on paper is a wonderful way to enhance your memory at a later date and remember just what you have seen at a given time. This is why mapping is such a rewarding project, one that can be accomplished by just one person or a whole group of people.

You will first want to decide on an area that intrigues you, one that you would like to become totally acquainted with. If you are making your map as an individual project, an 8½-by-14-inch sheet of paper will be sufficient in size; but if this project is being tackled by a large group or class, it would be more advisable to hang a large sheet of paper on the wall so all involved can add to it as time goes on.

Mapping can continue throughout an entire school year, one season, or one week, depending on the time you would like to invest. The initial investigation of an area is performed by the "mappers," who spend some time observing just what is in the area to be studied. Each person should be assigned to a particular area, which will be transcribed onto the large map that will hang on the wall for the duration of the project.

Everything observed in your area should be drawn and labeled on your map. During your first observation session draw any trees, bushes, buildings, anthills, birds passing over (identify them if you can!), spiders crawling by, and virtually everything that makes up the community of your map area. When the initial map is drawn you will already have quite a record of the life in this area.

As the days go by, each person should be constantly aware of what they see passing by and living in the mapped area. When something is observed, whether it is seen on the way to class, during lunch break, or whenever, always remember to add it to the map in the location in which it was seen. Each addition should be dated and initialed by the person who observed it.

This observation exercise can be continued as long as you would like, or until the map is so crammed full of information that a new one would need to be started.

Your finished product will be something each person involved will be quite proud of!

STORY TWISTS

What imaginations we all have—and a wonderful way to bring them out is by playing Story Twists with friends, family, and classmates. Everybody involved will be building a nature story that will always be different no matter how many times you rewrite it.

Each person should be given a pencil and piece of paper and asked to write down one line of a nature story. It can be the introduction, middle, climax, or ending of the story. They may write a line that says, "It wasn't long before the fox was seen dashing across the field," or "The poor bald owl fell six feet out of the tree!" All the nature sentences are folded up and placed in a bowl, bag, or the like. One person at a time is chosen to draw a paper out, reading the line on the sheet they have drawn. Go around the room, getting each person to draw out another piece of paper and reading what they have drawn. As you go, you will be building a usually funny and nonsensical nature story written by everyone in the group!

HELP NATURE'S COMMUNITY!

How do our towns and communities survive and prosper? By people helping each other—and nature's community works in much the same way. Without our help, there are times when it just can't survive and grow to its fullest potential.

Every place is unique and different from the next, making this a great time for your group to get out, sit down, and think of how you can help nature's community in your home towns.

You might find that litter is your big problem. If so, get your heads together and devise some ways to make your environment more attractive. Sometimes just picking it up might not be the only answer. Consider adding trash cans, friendly signs, or anything you think might be effective.

Maybe you have a really great trail in a nearby local park, but the ground is so badly eroded that it is crumbling away in steep areas along banks. Do you think your group would like to go out and repair it?

Possibly you live in a town that has very few trees and flowers to brighten it up. Try a group project to plant a few, or maybe set out some flowers or flowerboxes to bring nature's beauty to your neighborhood.

Wherever you live, if you look you will find nature's community has certain problems that your group can pitch in and help solve. Let's get involved and keep our natural environment a special number-one project on all our lists!

RECORDING MEMORIES

Keeping a Diary or Sketchbook

From day to day it can be difficult to remember what you did even the day before. Just imagine trying to remember what you may have observed on an outing a year ago!

Keeping a record of thoughts, memories, and observations is a fascinating way to keep track of where one has been and what was seen...and a lot of fun to pick up and read a year later.

Take your "windows" to the field and forests and you will be pleasantly surprised as you discover the smaller forms of life that flourish beneath our feet.

Students may ask: What do you put in a nature diary? Just about anything your heart desires. The only limit to your additions is your imagination. You may have taken a relaxing hike one Saturday afternoon and on the way observed several unusual wildflowers and birds, or gotten a great glimpse of some deer in the woods. This is the perfect thing to write down, with the date you observed them. Many folks like to add their feelings to a diary of this kind, the thrill they felt at seeing something they may never have seen before.

On one of your journeys you may encounter an absolutely beautiful spot, one that could be rekindled in your memory by a sketch of the scene you so enjoyed. Or maybe you could not identify one of those wildflowers you saw; if you sketched what it looked like, you might be able to find it in a field guide later.

For that matter, you don't need to go on an outing or a hike to have a reason to keep a diary. Try keeping one on the natural activities right in your own schoolyard. While you're at home working or maybe peering out the window on a rainy day, you never know what will fly by or what might catch your interest. The subject matter is limited only by what you choose to record and remember.

A Natural Workbook

Sometimes one's mind can draw a blank when first attempting to begin a nature diary or sketchbook. If you are working with a group, or with one of your children, introduce them to the idea of recording their thoughts by first beginning a natural workbook with them. By preparing a workbook, you introduce a series of already prepared worksheets that contain ideas for stimulating people to look more closely at the world around them. Try using some of the following ideas for your beginning worksheets, then begin making up some of your own. Whatever subject matter you want to explore can be incorporated into prearranged questions, drawings, and discovery ideas to help get started on your notebook.

CREATING A STORY

Anything that strikes your eye is a potential story topic. You may be impressed with something as small as a spider or a newly blooming wildflower, or as large as the grandeur of a towering oak or the coming of a winter snow.

The first step in writing a story is to choose a subject that most inspires you. Be relatively specific so your subject isn't too broad to handle.

This particular story is going to be a very special one, one that is very reflective. As you begin composing, think about the entire history of the topic you are writing about.

Begin by describing its past—what did it do, where was it before you discovered it? Just what type of life or preparation for life did this particular thing have?

After you have described the past, it is time to move on to the present. What are you seeing now? Why does this thing exist? What is its purpose in life? More important, why is this thing so special to you?

Finally, your story will project the future of your subject. What is its ultimate fate? Will it return to be seen again or pass on, leaving its offspring to continue its existence?

Depending on the subject matter you choose, many fascinating ideas and thoughts can be related in your special story. Make this a time for personal reflection, opening up your mind to the incredible changes that occur within just one organism in our environment.

Don't stop after one story, but continue writing them anytime you find some intriguing creature, place, or thing before your eyes.

CLOSING IN!

As you continue your explorations into the natural world, the quantity of discoveries can be overwhelming. It becomes hard to decide just what subject matter to choose for any particular activity, for everything seems just as wonderful as every other.

Zoom in for a closeup of some of your favorite places; doing this can bring out the wonder of the details that you may have passed by too quickly. Have a pencil and paper handy so you can record and sketch your observations. For instance, if you choose to close in on the bark of a tree, be prepared to sketch just what you are seeing. The closer you get, the more details will stand out.

Take a piece of paper, fold it in half, and cut out the center so you will have an open-centered square or rectangle when you're finished. In a sense, you will have a small window in your hand. As you travel with your personal window, concentrate only on what you are seeing within it, blocking your mind to the areas outside its borders. When you find the perfect view, lay your window down and closely study the details of the object that you have found with it. To record your observations, sketch the details of your subject.

To become further involved, you may want to make a series of smaller and smaller windows to carry around with you. You will then be prepared to get closer and closer as you discover the beautiful details of many living things.

NATURE IN VERSE

The art of reading and writing poetry is one of special feelings and memories. Listening to the flow of a descriptive piece of verse can take your mind into worlds hidden deep within our hearts.

Adding original pieces of poetry to our notebooks can give them a very special warmth; a warmth that makes the notebook an integral part of the writer and the natural world.

Writing a poem really isn't as difficult as you might think, especially if you follow a few easy guidelines and let the words flow from your heart. There are many different forms of poetry following a variety of cadences. If you choose the cadence you want to follow and add to that a few ideas for descriptions, the rest of the poem should come naturally.

The first step is to choose a subject that especially entices you; for instance, a thunderstorm, a new flower of spring, a drop of dew in the morning, or the emergence of a young bird from its egg.

After deciding on your subject, just follow the guidelines below and your poem will fall into place as gently as autumn leaves touching the ground.

Line 1	1 to 2 words	Tell what it is you're writing about
Line 2	3 words	Explain where it is
Line 3	4 to 5 words	What is it doing?
Line 4	3 words	What are you doing?
Line 5	1 to 2 words	How does it make you feel?

Some of my favorites have been written by students visiting Roan Mountain on field trips. Here are a couple of examples to give you an idea of what your imagination can do!

Storm clouds
Cresting the mountaintop
Floating quietly through the sky
Watching from below
Exploding within

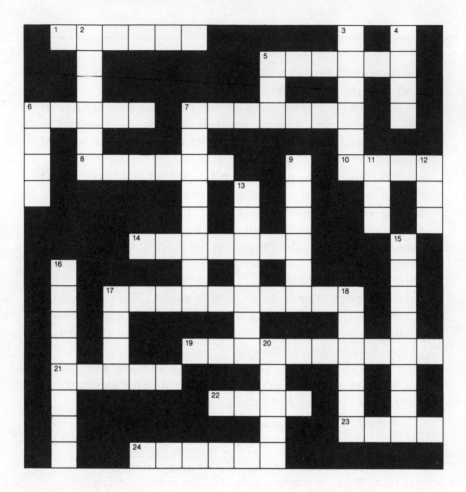

ACROSS

1 Plant growing on rocks and trees, part fungus, part alga.
5 The living things of our physical world.
6 Small stream.
7 A type of bird, Indigo _____.
8 Reptile with body enclosed in leathery shell.
10 A fertilized plant ovule capable of developing a new plant.
14 A small, often yellowish bird with colorful markings.
17 Large-billed bird that feeds on fish.
19 Plants characterized by seeds enclosed in ovary.
21 To become mature and fully developed.
22 Small burrowing animal.
23 Hoarfrost.
24 Dense growth of trees.

DOWN

2 Invertebrate with 3 pairs of legs and 3-segmented body.
3 A plant lacking chlorophyll.
4 Partially carbonized vegetable matter.
5 Hickory _____ (squirrel food).
6 Large black bird.
7 A "deep croaking" pond inhabitant.
9 Surface burn.
11 A shade tree.
12 A lair.
13 The act of losing feathers.
15 A plant with gills.
16 Small tree-climbing animal with a bushy tail.
17 A large seaweed.
18 Bird of prey.
20 Narrow passage of water.

Peepers
By the pond
Singing to the sky
Sitting, listening, watching
Free

NATURE'S SHAPES

For this page of your workbook, you will need to prepare a sheet that has four columns across the top. At the top of column 1 will be a drawing of a circle, column 2 will have a drawing of a square, column 3 will have a drawing of a triangle, and column 4 will have a rectangle.

With this sheet prepared, you can either use your memory and try to complete it indoors or head outside where you can look around, say on a field trip, on a walk down a trail, or on a drive in the car. Beneath each column list all the things you can think of in our natural world that are shaped like the geometric form at the head of the column. What things do you see that are circular? Square? Rectangular? Triangular? You'll find some harder than others, and will probably be thankful if you can go out and look for them. Which shape is the easiest to find in nature? You'll soon find out as you write the answers down under your individual columns. Use your imagination, too, for something circular can range from an animal hole in the ground to a drop of rain falling from the sky. What do you see that is square? Maybe you'll run across a square clump of dirt, who knows? Continue your hunt, filling in each column as you go. You're sure to be surprised at your results.

FOREST CROSSWORDS

Everyone loves to sit down with a good crossword puzzle once in a while, but have you ever thought of making up your own? It's not hard to do, and you can make it just as easy or difficult as you wish.

You can make up your own to give to anyone keeping a natural workbook or use the example below. Whichever you choose, you'll find a challenge in trying to answer the questions you have created as an addition to your ever-growing workbook. If you decide to write your own, there are a few easy ways to get started.

Try writing down words on a sheet of paper, choosing ones that you think you can make up some good questions about—words that have something to do with nature. Or, if you prefer, give your puzzle a specific theme, narrowing down your subject to one theme. Begin connecting your words, intertwining them just as you would do in playing a game of Scrabble. When you are finished you need to go back and number each across and down word, beginning on the top line and working your way to the bottom. It will be easier to look at the example than to try to explain it, so try to work out the following example. When you are finished you can use it as a model to write your own. The answers can be found upside down at the bottom, but don't peek until you've given it your best try!

These are but a few examples of what can comprise your workbook. Create your own original worksheets whenever something special strikes your fancy. Remember, there is no limit to the subjects you can explore. Our earth is full of an array of plants, animals, and natural wonders, from the tiny creatures within the soil clear to the stars. Drawings, stories, or even fact sheets can add interesting information to your book to be reread and enjoyed time and time again.

Epilogue
Rainbows and Revelations

It seems as though every little town and community you visit has a fascinating history or legend associated with it. Each one is totally unique and lends a great deal of character to its home.

There is a haunting legend of nature's mysterious ways that has graced Roan Mountain since the 1700s. This mountain is on the Tennessee–North Carolina border, resting at an elevation of 6285 feet. From the highest ridges, a "ghostly choir of angels" was heard by herdsmen and visitors to the old Cloudland Hotel, which in the late 1800s sat atop the Roan. This "mountain music," usually heard while thunderstorms were passing through the valleys below, was followed by the appearance of a circular rainbow at the lower elevations.

A young scientist by the name of Henry Colton had the opportunity to hear it himself while staying at the old Cloudland Hotel. From the hotel site, Mr. Colton and friends walked to the glen during a thunderstorm in the

Be it a rainbow or the gentle outline of the sun peeking out from behind a cloud, nature's beauty and changes will greet you every moment right at your own back door. (Photo by John Bryant)

valley. In search of a logical explanation for this mystery, Mr. Colton decided the following:

> But I only convinced myself that it was the result from two currents of air meeting each other in the suck between the two peaks where there was no obstruction of trees, one containing a greater, the other a lesser amount of electricity.

Who knows? Whatever the cause, I have always been fascinated by this phenomenon and the fact that during or after this "mountain music" a circular rainbow would appear. I had looked and listened hopefully for years, to no avail, but at last all my wildest dreams came true.

There was quite a ring of thunderstorms around the Roan. The sun would peek out, then another cloud would come along. I had planned an evening walk on the mountain, so I began driving with a friend to the top to see if it was raining above us.

The light was quite eerie, reflecting oranges, reds, and yellows, then turning dark and windy. All the way up the mountain the rain came down in a gentle, soaking shower.

Upon rounding one of the higher curves, the friend with me hollered, "Look at the rainbow!" As we stopped on the road we were delighted to see the most exquisite rainbow—our first *circular* rainbow! Not only was it circular, but as we gazed upon it, another grew almost miraculously in front of our very eyes, forming a double circular rainbow!

There we stood in that gentle rain for over thirty minutes, as if in a trance, finally seeing the circular rainbow that legend had told us about for years.

We have all had experiences that have seemed just as exciting, ones that during quiet times we have remembered with a smile. Why is it that what seems so very simple is actually so special to us? Why *do* we care about the rainbows?

Maybe it's the spontaneity of nature's way. Nothing is planned; we are always greeted with a surprise. Nature proceeds despite us; whether we existed or not, the wind would still blow and the flowers would still bloom.

Nature could continue and thrive without us, yet the presence of the human race sometimes puts a strain on the natural things of this earth. It is sad to think that there are those who continue to pollute our land. Our very lifestyle is one that produces waste; while we try to find better ways to dispose of it, the earth picks up the leftovers.

As the population grows and the demand increases for additional housing and space to live and shop, so our natural world continues to disappear by way of the bulldozer, one small chunk at a time.

That is why it is so very important for us to care, to love the trees and their kin, for it would be very easy to erase nature's kind from our planet if we do not slow down a moment, stop, and think.

From areas as immense as our national parks to the single tree in your own backyard, all are important to each and every one of us, both physically and for our peace of mind.

If it weren't for the forces of nature we would have no food, water, or fresh air to breathe. With each of these things being in a very delicate balance, so easily upset and confused by human action and pollution, we must consider carefully our actions and their effects on these forces.

We must protect and nurture the earth, both for ourselves and future generations, for in our hands we hold the knowledge to either destroy or protect it.

The activities in this book represent a beginning to reaching out and sharing with others our desire to preserve our environment. You may guide people of all ages a little

Just as the yellow ladies' slipper awakes with its curls and arises from the warm spring ground, so will each one of us as we let the earth's joys and mysteries become one with our lives.

closer to that childlike wonder each and every one of us possesses but sometimes forgets.

Think back to all those great memories you have of things that have happened to you on an outdoor excursion or even just outside your back door. Living quite a distance from the ocean, I've always remembered how exciting it was to walk along the beach, trying to dodge the waves as they flattened out and rolled in across the sand, only to end up wiggling my toes in the water anyway. The great thing about it is that it's just as much fun now as when I was a child going to the shore with my parents.

Whether you are young or old, your life can be filled with new memories every day of your life, as long as you keep your eyes open to the world around you. There is a small grayish bird called a phoebe that builds itself a cozy little nest every year under the roof of a building in the campground. For the last four years, like clockwork, the same boy comes back to check on his favorite bird. And every year as he returns and realizes the phoebe has survived the winter and once again is beginning a new nest, he hollers in delight at the start of another glorious season.

Share your thrill of life with others. You will find so many yearning for that special experience that you can guide them to. If you find yourself working with groups, you will soon notice that no two people are alike. Keep your eyes keen as to how they respond, what they like, and even what their fears are in studying nature.

Surroundings that are very familiar to you may be incredibly strange and maybe even frightening at first to some folks. Don't rush them into situations they are not ready for, as what may be comforting to one person may seem a threat to another. Folks from different backgrounds will have very different perspectives as to what nature is all about. It is easy to be cautious and sometimes fearful of something new. Lack of exposure can sometimes create a lack of understanding, which you as a guide can help change.

Where a person lives can make a big difference in how readily they accept the out-of-doors. I remember on one particular hike a woman who eagerly yearned to be in the forests and learn the ways of the mountains. It was new and really exciting to her, but she had lived in a large city all her life and had not until this day had the opportunity to head to the woods. About halfway through the hike she burst into tears, truly frightened in these strange surroundings. As soon as she realized she was just twenty steps from a nearby house, she felt better and soon became relaxed with her new environment. Now she returns to the mountains every year, and it seems as if she grew up right in the area that once scared her. As she began to realize that nature's way was the way that sustained her even at home in the city, she then began to accept the land as her friend.

Even though you may have experienced something many times before, never forget how great it was the first time, for someone else will always be coming along for their first time too. You, as their guide, can enhance their excitement or squelch it. Always enhance it by communicating your caring to others.

Use this book as a beginning to a lifetime of revelations. Don't stop here. . . .

🍁 Begin each day with a new eye to the life around you. Our world is overwhelming in its diversity. You may find yourself observing the deserts and their moisture-conserving species or by the ocean searching for a delicate seashell resting on the sand. You may journey to the mountains or the plains, or search within our towns and cities, daydreaming as the clouds pass overhead.

🍁 Every different place is unique in its ability to support its own special life forms in the climate they require. Explore all the great things, large and small, about these places. You can do this in books or by firsthand experience. This book of outside and inside activities can be adapted to any type of environment you wish to explore. Let us open the doors of the natural world for you.

🍁 Always remember that nature is right outside your doorway no matter where you live. Nearby trees are homes for a variety of birds, squirrels and chipmunks. Listen for the tiny screech owl in the spring; look around buildings for the nest of the phoebe; watch for a woodpecker hunting insects on the side of a tree; look to the skies for the flight of a hawk or the coming of a summer storm. Sit on your porch steps, close your eyes, and listen to the sounds of nature at its best.

🍁 As the seasons change, continue to record in your notebook all the marvelous things nature has shared with you in its changings.

🍁 Record in your memories those special moments— the baby bird craning its neck in search of its dinner, the quiet opening of a new flower, the changing of the moon on a crisp, clear night. All are an integral part of our very existence; you, as a guide to yourself and to others, hold the key to opening the eyes of people of all ages to the beauties and mysteries of nature's wonders.

Additional Reading

Within this bibliography you will find a varied selection of books and periodicals that will aid you in furthering your interest in the world of nature study. You will find field guides, magazines, books of an aesthetic nature, and books with more scientific information. Many of the books published prior to 1960 may be out of print, but are for the most part available in libraries or can be found by your local librarian. I urge you to seek out these books wherever possible, as you will find them very helpful and informative in your continued reading.

ESPECIALLY FOR THE YOUNGER FOLK

ADAMS, ADRIENNE. *Poetry of Earth*. New York: Scribners, 1972.

BEHNKE, FRANCES L. *What We Find When We Look Under Rocks*. New York: McGraw Hill, 1971.

BUCK, MARGARET WARING. *In Woods and Fields.* Cokesbury: Abingdon, 1950.

BUCK, MARGARET WARING. *In Yards and Gardens.* Cokesbury: Abingdon, 1952.

COOPER, ELIZABETH K. *Science in Your Own Backyard.* New York: Harcourt, 1958.

CROSBY, ALEXANDER L. *Junior Science Book of Pond Life.* New York: Garrard, Easton, 1964.

FULLER, RAYMOND TIFFT. *Nature Quests and Quizzes: A Nature Seeker's Handbook.* New York: J. Day Co., 1948.

HAMERSTROM, FRANCES. *Walk When the Moon Is Full.* New York: Crossing Press, 1975.

HOWELL, RUTH REA. *A Crack in the Pavement.* New York: Atheneum, 1970.

HUNTINGTON, HARRIET E. *Let's Go to the Brook.* New York: Junior Literary Guild and Doubleday, 1952.

HYLANDER, CLARENCE JOHN. *Out of Doors in Autumn.* New York: Macmillan, 1942.

HYLANDER, CLARENCE JOHN. *Out of Doors in Spring.* New York: Macmillan, 1942.

HYLANDER, CLARENCE JOHN. *Out of Doors in Summer.* New York: Macmillan, 1942.

HYLANDER, CLARENCE JOHN. *Out of Doors in Winter.* New York: Macmillan, 1943.

NICOL, LUCILLE. *The Nature Hour.* New York: Newark, Silver, Burdett, & Co. 1935.

PEATTIE, DONALD CULROSS. *Rainbow Book of Nature.* Willowstone Park: World Publishing, 1957.

RUSSELL, HELEN ROSS. *Small Worlds: A Field Trip Guide.* Boston: Little, Brown, 1972.

SIMON, SEYMOUR. *Science in a Vacant Lot.* New York: Viking, 1970.

Children's Nature Periodicals

CHICKADEE (preschool)
The Young Naturalist Foundation
59 Front St., E.
Toronto, Ontario, Canada M5E 1 B3

THE CURIOUS NATURALIST
Massachusetts Audubon Society
South Great Road
Lincoln, MA 01773

ODYSSEY MAGAZINE
Astromedia Corporation
625 E. St. Paul Avenue
P.O. Box 92788
Milwaukee, WI 53202

OWL
The Young Naturalist Foundation
59 Front St., E.
Toronto, Ontario, Canada M5E 1 B3

RANGER RICK'S NATURE MAGAZINE
National Wildlife Federation
1412 16th St., NW
Washington, DC 20036

WORLD
National Geographic Society
P.O. Box 2330
Washington, DC 20013

YOUR BIG BACKYARD (ages 3–5)
National Wildlife Federation
1412 16th St., NW
Washington, DC 20036

Nature Coloring Books

DOVER PUBLICATIONS
189 Varick Street
New York, NY 10014

TROUBADOR PRESS
385 Freemont
San Francisco, CA 94105

CENTER FOR ENVIRONMENTAL EDUCATION
1925 K. Street, NW
Washington, DC 20006

OTHER READINGS

ALLISON, LINDA. *Sierra Club Summer Book.* New York: Scribners, 1977.

ARNETT, ROSS H., AND RICHARD JACQUES. *Insect Life.* Englewood Cliffs, NJ: Prentice-Hall, Inc., 1985

BAGER, BERTEL. *Nature as Designer: A Botanical Art Study.* New York: Reinhold Publishing, 1966

BROWN, VINSON. *The Amateur Naturalist's Handbook.* Englewood Cliffs, NJ: Prentice-Hall, Inc.

CADUTO, *Pond and Brook.* Englewood Cliffs, NJ: Prentice-Hall, Inc., 1985.

CARSON, RACHEL. *The Sense of Wonder.* New York: Harper and Row, 1956.

COMSTOCK, ANNA (BOTSFORD). *Handbook of Nature Study.* New York: Comstock Publishing, 1939.

COON, NELSON. *The Dictionary of Useful Plants*. Emaus, PA Rodale Press, 1974.

DILLARD, ANNIE. *Pilgrim at Tinker Creek*. New York: Harper's Magazine Press, 1974.

FIAROTTA, PHYLLIS. *Snips and Snails and Walnut Whales: Nature Crafts for Children*. New York: Workman Publishing, 1975.

HEADSTROM, RICHARD. *Suburban Trilogy*. Englewood Cliffs, NJ: Prentice-Hall, Inc.

HEADSTROM, RICHARD. *Nature in Miniature*. New York: Knopf, 1968.

HILLMAN, RUTH. *Life Along the Fencerow*. Scottsdale, AZ: Herald Press, 1974.

KIRKLAND, WALLACE. *The Lure of the Pond*. Chicago, IL: Regnery-Gateway-Lake Bluff, 1969

KRUTCH, JOSEPH WOOD. *The Twelve Seasons: A Perpetual Calendar for the Country*. New York: Sloane Associates, 1949.

LARRICK, NANCY. *Room for Me and a Mountain Lion: Poetry of Open Space*. New York: M. Evans, 1974.

LESLIE, CLARE W. *Nature Drawing*. Englewood Cliffs, NJ: Prentice-Hall, Inc.

LEOPOLD, ALDO. *Round River*. New York: Oxford University Press, 1953.

LINK, MICHAEL. *Outdoor Education*. Englewood Cliffs, NJ: Prentice-Hall, Inc.

MILLER, ORSON K., JR. *Mushrooms of North America*. New York: E. P. Dutton, 1977.

MITCHELL, JOHN. *The Curious Naturalist*. Englewood Cliffs, NJ: Prentice-Hall, Inc., 1980.

NEEDHAM, PAUL R. *A Guide to the Study of Freshwater Biology*. San Francisco: Holden Day, 1962.

OGDEN, EUGENE C. *Field Guide to Northeastern Ferns. Bulletin*. #444. New York State Museum, State Education Dept., NY, 1981.

PEPI, DAVID. *Thoreau's Method*. Englewood Cliffs, NJ: Prentice-Hall, Inc., 1985.

RAYMO, *365 Starry Nights*. Englewood Cliffs, NJ: Prentice-Hall, Inc.

RUBLOWSKY, JOHN. *Nature in the City*. New York: Basic Books, 1967.

SARGENT, CHARLES S. *Manual of the Trees of North America*. (2 volumes.) New York: Dover Publications, 1965.

SHARPE, GRANT W., ED. *Interpreting the Environment*. New York: Wiley, 1976.

SISSON, EDITH. *Nature with Children of All Ages*. Englewood Cliffs, NJ: Prentice-Hall, Inc., 1982.

SYMONDS, GEORGE W. D. *The Shrub Identification Book*. New York: Wm. Morrow & Co., 1958.

SYMONDS, GEORGE W. D. *The Tree Identification Book*. New York: Wm. Morrow & Co., 1958.

TILDEN, FREEMAN. *Interpreting Our Heritage*. Chapel Hill, NC: University of North Carolina Press, 1977.

VINAL, WILLIAM GOULD. *Nature Recreation: Group Guidance for the Out of Doors*. New York and London: McGraw Hill, 1940.

VINAL, WILLIAM GOULD. *Nature Guiding*. New York: Comstock, 1926.

FIELD GUIDES

A good selection of the following field guide series can be found in most bookstores.

GOLDEN GUIDES
Western Publishing Co.
866 3rd Ave.
New York, NY 10022

AUDUBON NATURE GUIDES
Doubleday and Co.
501 Franklin St.
Garden City, NY 11530

PETERSON'S FIELD GUIDES
Houghton Mifflin Co.
2 Park Street
Boston, MA 02107

RECORDINGS

THE PETERSON FIELD GUIDE SERIES. *A Field Guide to Bird Songs of Eastern and Central North America.* Boston: Houghton Mifflin Co., 1971.

BARROR, DONALD J. *Bird Songs and Bird Behavior.* New York: Dover Publications, 1972.

BARROR, DONALD J. *Songs of Eastern Birds.* New York: Dover Publications, 1970.

ASTRONOMY

Especially recommended sources of information:

MCDONALD OBSERVATORY NEWS
University of Texas
Dept. of Astronomy
Austin, TX 78712

HANSEN PLANETARIUM
Space Science Library and Museum
15 South State Street
Salt Lake City, UT 84111

ASTRONOMY MAGAZINE
Astromedia Corporation
625 E. St. Paul Avenue
P.O. Box 92788
Milwaukee, WI 53202

SCIENCE NEWS MAGAZINE
Science Service
1719 N. St., NW
Washington, DC 20036

Index
